MINDFUL FUTURES: CHAOS TO CLARITY

A Self-Help Transformational Guide to Managing Expectations and Discovering Happiness to Unlock Growth, Inner Peace, and Success

NAVNEET CHANDRA

Clever Fox® PUBLISHING
Chennai • Bangalore

CLEVER FOX PUBLISHING
Chennai, India

Published by CLEVER FOX PUBLISHING 2025

ISBN: 978-93-6707-880-8

To my First Guru – My Father :

Late Shri N. C. Kulshrestha...

CONTENTS

PREFACE

The Moment I Knew Expectations Needed Rewriting

It was 1982. The ink on my exam results was still fresh when I learned my first painful lesson about expectations. I had done well, really well, but the faces around me told a different story. My parents' hesitant smiles, my uncle's thoughtful sigh, and the way my aunt immediately asked about the neighbour's son's marks. Their silent chorus of *"You could have done better"* drowned out my own quiet pride.

Thirty-two years later, history repeated itself - but this time, I held the pen.

When my son received his exam results in 2014, I watched his shoulders slump as he compared his good scores to his friends' excellent ones. In that moment, I remembered 1982 with perfect clarity. So I did something radical for a parent in our achievement-obsessed culture: I publicly celebrated him exactly as he was.

My Facebook post on 29th May 2014 - "I set my elder son Nishant Kulshrestha a target for his class 12 exams...

He exceeded it!!! That's what matters... NOT whether he got above 90% or what percentage he got... TARGET ACHIEVED and EXCEEDED!!!!! Well done, Nishant!!— Feeling excited."

The Facebook post was simple - just a proud parent's words tagged to his profile. But the reaction was extraordinary. Friends and family automatically assumed he must have topped his class (he hadn't). More importantly, I watched my son straighten his posture and reclaim his joy right before my eyes.

That was when I knew:

We don't have an achievement gap in our society. We have an expectation gap.

This book is my answer to that younger version of myself clutching his exam results, and to every parent, professional, and dreamer who's ever had their joy hijacked by someone else's "should."

This book grew from a simple, human question: *Why do our achievements sometimes taste like loss?* Not because we're ungrateful. Not because we didn't work hard enough. But somewhere between our hopes and reality, we forgot to ask the most important question:

Who decided this was supposed to make me happy?

What you'll find here

This isn't a manifesto against ambition. It's a compassionate exploration of:

- The silent expectations we carry without realising
- Why fulfilment often hides in unexpected places
- How to hold your dreams gently enough to let them breathe
- Why do we measure ourselves against invisible standards
- How to separate healthy motivation from toxic expectation
- The surprising neuroscience behind why expectations hurt
- Practical ways to protect your joy in an achievement-obsessed world

We'll walk through psychology and personal stories, but never at the expense of your dignity. No shaming. No "shoulds." Just honest conversation about why we chase what we chase, and how to do it with our eyes open.

A Note Before We Begin

Some of these pages might comfort you like a conversation with an old friend. Others may stir up questions you've been avoiding. That's okay. Growth isn't about having all the answers—it's about learning to ask better questions.

Some of these truths may comfort you. Some may challenge you. But all of them will help you rewrite the silent rules that have been running your life.

So make yourself some tea, maybe a drink or some chips to nibble on. Find a comfortable chair and let's talk about the space between what we imagine and what is real, and how to find yourself in that space .

The journey begins with a simple choice: Will you keep chasing someone else's finish line, or will you plant your own flag?

Let's find out together.

Navneet Chandra

FOREWORD

Brief explanation of the book's approach

This isn't just another book on managing expectations. No fluff. No overused self-help jargon. Just real insights, real strategies, and real results. Think of it as a conversation with a trusted mentor,- the kind who challenges you to think deeper, questions the obvious, and takes action.

Expect stories that sound familiar, examples that hit home, and analysis that makes you pause and rethink. Because expectations aren't just passive thoughts in our heads, - they shape every decision, every reaction, every win, and every heartbreak.

We'll start at the root, - how the brain processes expectations, the sneaky ways belief systems form, and how neurotransmitters dictate whether you feel hopeful or frustrated.

Spoiler alert: Most of our expectations aren't even ours. They're shaped by culture, upbringing, and past experiences - sometimes good, sometimes messy.

Then, we'll get personal. Ever felt gutted when something didn't go as planned? That's not just disappointment; it's your brain flagging a perceived failure. We'll dissect the emotional rollercoaster of unmet expectations, the hidden mechanics of self-sabotage, and how emotional intelligence can flip the script.

And yes, we're going into some tough matters - trauma, psychological complexes, and the silent assumptions that control our views on success, relationships, and self-worth. Most of us don't even realise how much our past dictates what we expect from the future. That changes here.

But it's not all deep dives and analysis. This book is packed with practical tools - mindfulness techniques, resilience hacks, and communication strategies. Everything that you need to set, express, and manage expectations in a way that drives growth instead of disappointment. Real-life case studies. Exercises that work. No theory without action.

Now, why does this matter? Because, despite expectations being the single most powerful factor in our pursuit of happiness and fulfilment, no one has truly tackled them holistically. We have books on success, emotional intelligence, and resilience, but nothing that puts the whole system together. Meanwhile, a global crisis of discontent is brewing-frustration, burnout, shattered illusions. It's time to stop the negative tsunami before it sweeps us under.

The goal? By the last page, you won't just understand expectations-you'll know how to master them. You'll know how to set expectations that propel you forward, communicate them in ways that get results, and handle let-downs without breaking stride. You'll stop letting expectations control you and start making them work for you.

If you're ready to take charge of your expectations - and by extension, your life - let's dive in.

INTRODUCTION: THE EXPECTATION GAME

ALWAYS REACHING, NEVER ARRIVING!

Ever felt like life is dangling a carrot just out of reach? No matter how hard you run, the finish line keeps moving. You get the promotion, but now there's a bigger title to chase. You hit your fitness goal, yet suddenly it's not enough. You finally take that dream vacation, but now your Instagram feed makes you want another one.

Welcome to the **Expectation Game** - where the rules are unclear, the goalposts keep shifting, and frustration is the prize for playing.

But here's the thing - you're not alone. Every 'thinking' being, from a corporate CEO to a squirrel hoarding nuts for winter, wrestles with expectations. They shape our ambitions, fuel our drive, and when reality doesn't match up, it dropkicks us into disappointment.

The problem isn't expectations themselves. The problem is 'how we manage them'. The wider the gap between what we expect and what actually happens, the more frustration creeps in. But this is where things get interesting and complicated at the same time. Remember the gap we were talking about? Well, it's also where 'growth happens'.

Understanding expectations, managing them, and learning to navigate their impact isn't just a skill - it's the key to sanity, success, and self-fulfilment. At the end of the day, expectations can either break us or push us to level up.

The Power of Expectations - The Script We Never Wrote

From the moment we open our eyes to the world, a script is handed to us. Not by choice, but by default.

Parents, teachers, society, everyone has a version of how life should go and should be. Study hard. Land a great job. Build the perfect life. Success means money, status, stability, and maybe even a house with a fancy nameplate. Follow the script, and happiness is guaranteed.

Or so they say.

But what happens when life doesn't stick to the script? When the dream job turns into a daily grind? When relationships don't look like the ones in those feel - good movies? When you check all the right boxes and still feel something's missing?

Frustration. Resentment. Self-doubt.

That gap between what we expect and what actually happens! That's where stress thrives, the more rigid our expectations, the harder the fall when reality refuses to cooperate.

But here's the twist, 'Managing expectations isn't about settling for less'. It's about aligning them with reality, staying flexible, and knowing when to double down or when to pivot. Because life doesn't always follow the script. Sometimes, you have to write your own.

The Hustle Trap - 'When More Is Never Enough'

Welcome to the age of more - More success. More wealth. More recognition. More hustle.

Somewhere along the way, we started believing that "enough" is never enough. That if we're not constantly achieving, growing, and outperforming, we're falling behind. Social media fuels it. Corporate culture reinforces it. Even personal relationships aren't immune to it. The result? We measure our worth against curated highlight reels, chasing a finish line that keeps moving.

Let's look at three common scenarios to understand this whole Hustle Trap clearly.

<u>Sarah - The Overachiever's Dilemma</u>

Sarah, a marketing executive, did everything right. Late nights, extra effort, exceeded targets, she expected a promotion. But when it went to someone else, she was crushed. Her work felt invisible. Her motivation vanished. She started questioning her worth, her abilities, even her future at the company.

<u>David - The Start-up Dream That Turned into a Nightmare</u>

David, an ambitious entrepreneur, launched his start-up expecting rapid success. Customers pouring in, investors lining up, his name in industry magazines. Instead? Delays. Rejections. Financial strain. The excitement turned into anxiety. Doubt crept in. Sleepless nights became the norm. Had he made a terrible mistake?

<u>Priya - The Pressure Cooker of Perfection</u>

Priya, a project manager, had everything planned: tight deadlines, a well-structured rollout, and a confident team. Then reality hit: unexpected glitches, resource shortages, and last-minute client demands. The delays frustrated her. The pressure got to her. She snapped at her team. Morale took a hit. The weight of expectations crushed her confidence.

<u>Different stories. Same struggle.</u>

We expect the world to reward effort with outcomes, but life doesn't always work that way. The real problem is not the hustle - it's the expectations we attach to it.

Embracing the Unexpected - The Art of Navigating Life's Curveballs

Life has a wicked sense of humour. Just when you think you've got everything figured out - BAM! - A curveball straight to the face. A missed opportunity. A sudden setback. A plan that unravels just when it was coming together.

The goal isn't to dodge them. That's impossible. The key is to anticipate, adapt, and grow.

The more we cling to rigid expectations, the harder the fall when things don't go our way. But when we learn to adjust, to let go of the how it should have been, and embrace what is, something shifts. We stop resisting. We start evolving.

Managing expectations isn't about lowering them - it's about aligning them. Ambition with reality. Effort with patience. Striving with gratitude. Because expectations don't just shape what we aim for, they define how we experience the journey.

Success isn't just about meeting expectations. It's about knowing which ones to chase, which ones to tweak, and which ones to let go. Master that, and life stops feeling like a series of disappointments, and starts feeling like a series of opportunities.

Managing Expectations: Train the Muscle, Master the Game

Managing expectations isn't just a mindset - it's a skill, like muscle. The more you use it, the stronger it becomes. And like any workout, the right technique matters.

So, how do we start, or rather, where do we start? Well, that's simple! We start with ourselves.

Know the Real You

Forget what the world expects from you. What do you expect from yourself? Strip away the noise, society's checklists, family pressures, social media illusions. Define success on your terms. What truly matters to you? What makes you feel fulfilled?

☑ Reality Check your Expectations

Be ambitious, but be honest. Are your expectations realistic, or are they setting you up for frustration? Perfection, instant results, and guaranteed outcomes? That's a fantasy, not a strategy. The trick is to dream big while keeping your expectations flexible enough to evolve.

☑ Stay Adaptable

Life isn't a straight road, it's a maze with detours, roadblocks, and surprise shortcuts. The most successful people aren't the ones who never stumble; they're the ones who know how to pivot when the plan falls apart. Adaptability isn't just helpful, it's essential.

☑ Practice Gratitude

Happiness isn't about having more and more, it's about appreciating what you already have. Celebrate the small wins. Acknowledge progress, even if it's not where you thought you'd be by now. Gratitude shifts your focus from what's missing to what's already here, making unmet expectations feel like stepping stones, not dead ends.

☑ Build Resilience

Setbacks will happen. That's a given. What matters is what you do next. Do you let disappointment define you, or do you use it to refine you? Resilience is about learning, adjusting, and moving forward, not getting stuck in the gap between expectation and reality.

Master these and expectations, stop being roadblocks. They become guides, shaping you into someone who can handle whatever life throws next.

THE BRAIN

THE HIDDEN ARCHITECT OF OUR EXPECTATIONS

The Subway Ride That Changed Everything

Imagine stepping onto a subway (Metro in some parts of the world), exhausted after a long day. You expect a smooth, quiet ride home. But the moment you sit, a man rushes in with two young children, who immediately start yelling, running, and disturbing everyone around them.

Annoyed, you glare at the father. How irresponsible. Why isn't he controlling his kids?

Finally, you snap. "Can you please get them to behave?"

The man looks up, dazed, as if waking from a dream. "I'm sorry," he mutters. "We just came from the hospital. Their mother passed away an hour ago. I don't know how to handle it, and neither do they."

Everything changes in an instant.

Your frustration evaporates. Your perception shifts. What seemed like chaos now looks like grief. And just like that, your expectations of the man, of the situation, were rewritten.

Now, ask yourself: How often does your brain misjudge situations because of pre-set expectations?

That is the power of your brain. It builds a version of reality before you even fully experience it. But how? And can we change the way it operates?

The Brain's Blueprint: How It Constructs Expectations

Our brain is not a single, all-knowing machine. It's a network of specialised players, each with a unique role in shaping how we predict, react, and navigate life. Think of it like an orchestra, one section plays too loudly, and the entire symphony changes. To understand better, let's look at this orchestra one section at a time.

The Prefrontal Cortex: The CEO of Predictions

Right behind your forehead sits the Cortex - your mental control tower. It makes predictions, strategies, and adapts based on past experiences.

It calculates outcomes: "Will this conversation go well?"

It sets expectations: "If I do X, Y should happen."

It corrects mistakes: "That didn't go as planned - adjust strategy."

A strong, flexible prefrontal cortex means you can adjust expectations in real time. A rigid one? It clings to old patterns, leading to repeated disappointments.

The Limbic System: The Emotional Editor

While the prefrontal cortex predicts, the limbic system decides how you feel about those predictions.

The Amygdala sounds alarms when expectations are shattered.

The Hippocampus stores emotional memories, influencing future predictions.

The Hypothalamus converts expectations into physical responses, such as stress, relief, and frustration.

If you've ever felt an instant emotional reaction when things didn't go as planned, that's your limbic system pulling the strings.

The Basal Ganglia: The Habit Enforcer

Your basal ganglia are like an old-school librarian - filing past experiences and retrieving them when needed.

If past meetings have ended badly, you expect tension before a new one even starts.

If you've been consistently praised, you anticipate positive feedback before it's given.

But here's the catch: the basal ganglia hates change. It clings to past experiences, reinforcing the same expectations, even when they no longer serve you.

The Thalamus: The Gatekeeper of Reality

Every second, your senses flood your brain with information. The thalamus decides what matters.

If you expect someone to be rude, your brain highlights their worst traits.

If you believe an event will fail, you unconsciously seek signs of failure.

This is why expectations shape reality. Before you even experience something, your brain has already decided what it should look like.

How the Brain's Shortcuts Reinforce Expectations

Imagine walking into a dark room. You see a curled-up shape in the corner. Your brain fills in the missing details.

Perhaps a rope? A jacket? A snake?

Your past experiences determine what you expect. If you've encountered a snake before, your brain triggers fear before confirming the truth.

This predictive mechanism is essential to keep you alive. But in modern life, it also creates cognitive biases that reinforce flawed expectations.

Confirmation Bias: We look for evidence that matches what we expect, and ignore what contradicts it.

Negativity Bias: The brain remembers failures more vividly than successes, leading to pessimistic predictions.

Anchoring Effect: The first piece of information we receive, colours everything that follows. This is why expectations often become self-fulfilling prophecies.

If you expect to fail, your brain focuses on obstacles. If you expect success, it highlights opportunities.

The Chemistry of Expectation: Neurotransmitters at Work

Beyond circuits and predictions, there's another force at play - brain chemistry. Neurotransmitters are the chemical messengers that shape how we perceive, predict, and react.

Dopamine: The Anticipation Drug

Dopamine is often called the "pleasure chemical," but that's only half the story. It doesn't just reward us, it fuels our expectations.

It surges before a reward arrives, keeping us motivated.

If the expectation is met, dopamine reinforces the behaviour.

If the expectation is broken, dopamine crashes, leading to disappointment.

Ever wonder why a near-win feels worse than a total loss? It's because dopamine was already released in anticipation, making the let-down sharper.

Serotonin: The Optimism Regulator

Serotonin stabilises expectations by influencing mood.

High serotonin = Confidence, positive outlook.

Low serotonin = Doubt, negative assumptions.

Chronic stress depletes serotonin, making pessimism the default. But activities like exercise, social connection, and mindfulness boost serotonin, making positive expectations easier.

Cortisol: The Disappointment Amplifier

Cortisol is the stress hormone. When expectations fail, cortisol floods the system, triggering frustration, anxiety, or even anger.

If cortisol levels stay high, the brain begins expecting negative outcomes as a survival mechanism. This explains why chronic stress rewires the brain for pessimism.

Oxytocin: The Trust Builder

Oxytocin shapes social expectations.

When oxytocin is high, we expect kindness and connection.

When low, we become sceptical and guarded.

This is why betrayal from a loved one stings more than a stranger's insult.

Oxytocin had strengthened the expectation of trust.

Neuroplasticity: Changing Expectations by Rewiring the Brain

Here's the good news: Expectations are not permanent. Your brain is plastic, meaning it rewires itself based on new experiences and conscious effort.

Negative thought loops reinforce pessimism. New experiences force the brain to adjust, breaking old patterns. This means expectations can be reprogrammed.

How to Reshape Expectations

Challenge rigid beliefs: Ask, "Is this expectation based on fact or habit?"

Expose yourself to new experiences: The brain learns best through real-world proof.

Use repetition: The more you think a certain way, the more your brain hardwires it.

Understanding the Brain, Mastering Expectations

Your brain doesn't just see reality - it constructs it.

Every second, your senses take in about 11 million bits of information, but your brain can only process around 50 of them consciously. So what happens to the rest?

Your brain filters out the "unnecessary" details and focuses only on what it expects to be relevant.

Here's how the process unfolds:

Sensory Input floods in. Primary inputs of light, sound , touch, smell, and taste bombard your brain. **The Thalamus filters it.** It decides what's important and discards the rest. **Patterns Are Matched**. Your brain compares new input to past experiences, filling in gaps where needed. The result?

You don't perceive reality - you perceive an edited version of it, based on your expectations.

This is why: You "hear" your name in a noisy room, even if no one said it. You assume someone is annoyed if they send a short text. You see what you expect to see, not necessarily what's there.

Expectations shape perception. And perception, in turn, reinforces expectations. Your expectations shape reality. But reality isn't fixed, it's created in the mind.

By understanding the brain's predictive nature, questioning outdated assumptions, and rewiring faulty patterns, you can reshape how you experience the world.

The brain may be wired to predict, but you have the power to rewrite the script.

OUR BELIEF SYSTEMS

THE INVISIBLE FRAMEWORK SHAPING OUR LIVES

What you believe isn't just a thought, it's the lens through which you see the world. It dictates your expectations, fuels your decisions, and shapes how you handle success or failure. Your belief system is the quiet puppeteer pulling the strings, influencing everything from career moves to relationships.

Take Susan, for instance. A high-performing professional, she believed asking for help was a sign of weakness, an idea she absorbed from her overachieving family. So, she worked longer hours, took on too much, and refused to delegate. Her expectation? That she had to solve every problem by herself. The result? Burnout, frustration, and an exhausting cycle of self-sabotage.

Beliefs are mental shortcuts. They help us interpret life, but they also create blind spots. Some push us forward. Others chain us down. If you believe failure is a stepping stone, you embrace challenges. But if you believe failure defines your worth, you avoid risks at all costs. The trick?

Understanding which beliefs shape your expectations, and deciding whether they deserve to stay.

Ever watched someone hesitate at the edge of a diving board, convinced they'll belly flop? That's a limiting belief in action. It's not reality - it's a mental script, written by past experiences and reinforced over time.

Lisa was told as a child that she wasn't 'math smart.' So, even as an adult, she avoids anything with numbers, convinced she'll fail. But was she really bad at math, or did one bad grade shape a lifetime of self-doubt?

Raj grew up hearing "Men don't show weakness." Now, he struggles to express emotions, fearing judgment. He wears stress like armour, but deep down, it drains him. One belief, picked up years ago, still dictates his life.

The real danger of limiting beliefs? They don't just hold you back, they convince you the cage is locked, when in reality, the door was never shut.

How Beliefs Take Root (and Tighten Their Grip)

Beliefs don't just pop into existence. They are built, brick by brick, over time-crafted by experiences, upbringing, and social influences.

Childhood: The First Blueprints

Our earliest beliefs come from parents, teachers, and authority figures. A child raised hearing "Money is scarce" or "You must be perfect to succeed" internalises these messages, setting the stage for how they perceive the world.

Ravi grew up hearing, "Good boys don't question authority." Over time, he stopped speaking up, even when he had great ideas. His belief? That challenging opinions would bring punishment. The result was that Ravi missed quite a few opportunities, and his career went into a state of stagnation.

Meanwhile, Maya's parents celebrated mistakes as learning opportunities. She was encouraged to try, fail, and try again. As an adult, she embraced challenges, knowing failure isn't the end, just a stepping stone. How do you think her life fared? Well, she would have had more satisfaction and would surely succeed. And in comparison to Ravi, her life would be more stress-free and accomplished.

Experience: Repetition Reinforces Reality

Beliefs grow stronger when life keeps reinforcing them. A job seeker facing constant rejection might start believing, "I'm just not good enough." Over time, this belief solidifies, leading them to stop applying for opportunities, even ones they're qualified for.

Priya was always the last to be picked for sports teams. Over the years, she convinced herself she was unathletic. Now, as an adult, she avoids any physical activity, not because she lacks ability, but because an old belief whispers, "This isn't for you."

<u>Society: The Silent Sculptor</u>

Culture, media, and social norms shape our beliefs in ways we don't always notice. A society that glorifies hustle culture embeds the idea that "Rest is for the weak." Movies and ads paint rigid standards of beauty, success, and happiness. And if everyone around us echoes the same thoughts, we absorb them without question.

Arjun grew up watching men handle finances while women managed the home. So, despite his wife being financially savvy, he unconsciously expected to take charge of their money matters. Only when she confronted him, did he realise his belief wasn't based on reason - it was inherited.

<u>The Brain's Dirty Trick: Confirmation Bias</u>

Once a belief takes hold, your brain fights to keep it. Confirmation bias makes you notice things that align with your beliefs while filtering out contradictions. If you believe "People are selfish," you'll see every act of selfishness but overlook acts of generosity.

Mark pitched an idea at work. It was dismissed. That single rejection morphed into a belief: "My ideas aren't valuable." Over time, he stopped speaking up in meetings, convinced he had nothing worthwhile to contribute. The cycle repeated until this belief became his reality.

Why Changing Beliefs Feels Uncomfortable

Beliefs aren't just thoughts, they carry emotional weight. Changing them feels unsettling because it shakes up our identity. If someone has built their self-worth around being "the strong one," they may resist the idea that asking for help is okay. Recognising this emotional attachment is key to reshaping our beliefs.

Breaking Free: Rewriting the Mental Script

So, how do we shift limiting beliefs? Well, to be truthful, it's not an easy affair because you would be fighting your own self. It's an internal battle, but it can be done. Sometimes you might need external support to do it, but the basic fundamental steps stay the same.

Step 1: Identify the Belief

Ask yourself: What do I truly, with conviction, believe about this situation? Where did this belief come from? Would I hold the same belief if a friend were in my shoes?

Example: If you think, "I'll never be good at public speaking," ask why? Did one bad presentation in college cement this idea? A single misstep doesn't define your future.

Step 2: Find the Contradictions

Challenge confirmation bias. Hunt for evidence that proves your belief wrong. If you believe you're terrible at networking, remember a time you had a great conversation with someone new. If you think you're bad at leadership, recall a time you successfully guided a team, or a project.

Step 3: Reframe the Narrative

Swap limiting beliefs for empowering ones. Instead of, "I'm bad at public speaking," try "I'm learning to improve my speaking skills." Instead of "I always fail," say, "Every failure teaches me something valuable." Small shifts, massive impact.

Step 4: Act As If

Pretend the new belief is already true. If you want to believe, "I am confident in meetings," make a point to speak up, even if just once. If you want to believe, "I handle stress well," take on a small challenge. Each small win weakens the old belief and strengthens the new one.

Step 5: Surround Yourself with Growth-Minded People

The voices around you shape your beliefs. Spend time with people who challenge and motivate you. Read books, listen to podcasts, and engage with content that reinforces empowering beliefs.

Your Mind, Your Rules

Beliefs aren't permanent. They can be questioned, reshaped, and rewritten. The first step? Realising that expectations are often just reflections of old programming. Change the belief, and you change the expectation. Change the expectation, and you change the outcome.

Think of it as updating your mental software. Just because an outdated program has been running for years doesn't mean it should dictate your future. The power to rewrite your script? It's in your hands.

EMOTIONS

WHEN YOUR MIND WRITES A SCRIPT, LIFE WON'T FOLLOW

You've spent weeks perfecting a presentation. Late nights, endless rehearsals, a vision of roaring applause in your mind. But then? Just few polite nods. No thunderous claps, no beaming faces. Just an underwhelming, lukewarm response. What happens next? Disappointment, frustration, maybe even self-doubt, creeping in like an uninvited guest.

This is the emotional weight of expectations. They aren't just logical predictions, they're emotional investments. When reality aligns with what we expect, we feel elated, validated, and at peace. But when reality betrays our expectations, emotions flare, anger, sadness, even resentment.

Psychologists call this the expectation - reality gap, and it's a powerful trigger for emotional reactions. Studies show unmet expectations are one among the biggest sources of stress and conflict. Whether in friendships, workplaces, or customer service. A boss assumes their team will 'just get it.' A friend expects unconditional support. A customer demands perfection. When expectations aren't met, emotions surge.

But here's the twist - Emotions don't just react to expectations; they shape them, too. If you're feeling optimistic, you expect the best. If you're anxious, you brace for the worst. It's a self-feeding cycle, one that can either set you up for success or send you spiralling into frustration.

Take a naturally enthusiastic team leader. They assume their team shares their energy and commitment, so they set ambitious deadlines. When the team doesn't deliver, frustration kicks in. But had they recognised their emotional bias, they could have set more balanced expectations, and avoided unnecessary stress.

Or think of a student who pours hours into studying, expecting a top grade. When the result falls short, emotions take over: anger, sadness, maybe even shame. But by reassessing whether their expectations were realistic, they can shift from disappointment to growth.

Emotional Intelligence: The Secret Weapon for Managing Expectations

Enter emotional intelligence (EQ). Not a buzzword. Not a trendy concept. A game-changer. It's what separates great leaders from mediocre ones, stable relationships from turbulent ones, and inner peace from chronic frustration.

Daniel Goleman, the man who brought EQ into the spotlight, broke it down into five core components:

Self-awareness – Recognising when and how our emotions play a significant role in setting our expectations.

Self-regulation – Controlling how we react when expectations fall short.

Motivation – Focusing on long-term growth rather than short-term disappointments.

Empathy – Understanding and factoring in others' expectations.

Social skills – Communicating expectations clearly to prevent misalignment.

Think of an emotionally intelligent manager. Instead of assuming their team will 'figure it out,' they set clear expectations from the start. If someone falls short, they don't lash out-they address it constructively. Compare that to a manager who stays vague, reacts emotionally, and blames others. One builds trust; the other breeds resentment.

The same logic applies to personal relationships. A partner who communicates their emotional needs is far better at handling unmet expectations than one who stews in silence. EQ isn't about suppressing emotions; - it's about using them wisely.

Picture a couple planning a vacation. One expects a detailed itinerary; the other prefers spontaneity. If they don't communicate, frustration is inevitable. But if they acknowledge their emotional triggers and discuss their expectations, they can find a balance before the trip turns into a battleground.

Even friendships aren't immune. One friend expects constant availability, while the other has their own life to juggle. When expectations are mismatched, emotions escalate. Recognising these triggers can help recalibrate expectations before they damage relationships.

Taming Emotional Reactions: Three Powerful Strategies

So, what do you do when reality is quite different from what you had expected, when reality and expectations are nowhere near each other? Well, for starters, you can try these three battle-tested strategies.

Name It Before You Blame It

Emotions hit hard when expectations shatter. But before you react, pause. Ask yourself: What exactly am I feeling? Anger? Disappointment? Frustration? A Harvard study found that simply labelling emotions reduces their intensity, making it easier to respond rationally instead of impulsively.

Let's say your boss doesn't acknowledge your hard work. Your gut reaction? They don't value me! But if you pause and identify your true emotion, feeling unappreciated - you can address it logically instead of letting resentment fester.

Parents see this all the time. A child expects a reward for good behaviour, but doesn't get it. Disappointment turns into tears or tantrums. Teaching kids to name their emotions helps them manage their expectations, and avoid emotional meltdowns.

Adjust Expectations in Real Time

Rigid expectations are a recipe for disaster. When things go sideways, ask: Was my expectation realistic? Can I adjust it without compromising what truly matters?

Take a project deadline that gets missed. Instead of spiralling into frustration, shift your focus: What's salvageable? What can I learn for next time? Or consider a client expecting instant responses from a service provider. If they adjust their expectations to allow reasonable response times, they avoid unnecessary stress.

Even in social settings, people expect immediate replies to messages. Delays trigger anxiety. But adjusting to expectations, understanding that people have lives outside of their phones, can prevent unnecessary frustration.

Communicate. Clearly. Early. Often.

Most emotional conflicts aren't caused by reality; they're caused by unspoken or misaligned expectations. The solution? Communicate to them upfront.

Instead of assuming your colleague will handle a task 'the right way,' define what that means. Instead of expecting your partner to 'just know' what upsets you, talk about it before resentment builds.

Take a workplace example. A manager assumes their team knows overtime is expected during crunch time. The team, unaware, clocks out at normal hours. Frustration erupts. If the expectation had been communicated early, conflict could have been avoided. Clear expectations minimise emotional turbulence.

Managing expectations isn't just about adjusting what we expect from others, -it's about mastering our emotional responses to the unexpected. The more emotionally intelligent we become, the better we get at setting, managing, and recalibrating expectations. And the less likely we are to let disappointment derail our progress.

Because at the end of the day, expectations will always exist. The real question is: How will you handle what happens next?

TRAUMA

THE SHOCK THAT REWRITES REALITY

Trauma is a thief. It sneaks in, uninvited, and steals safety, trust, and certainty. It doesn't just bruise the heart - it rewires the mind. It shapes how people see the world, and more importantly, how they expect the world to treat them.

So, what exactly is trauma?

At its core, trauma is an emotional wound. A deep, often invisible scar left by distress or life-altering events. It can be a single moment of terror, a car accident, an assault, or perhaps years of slow erosion, neglect, abuse, or chronic stress. The American Psychological Association calls trauma an "emotional response to a terrible event." But let's be honest: trauma isn't about the event itself. It's about the aftermath. The lingering fear. The subconscious rewiring. The new, often painful, expectations it leaves behind.

The Many Faces of Trauma

Acute Trauma – One catastrophic event that shakes the foundation. A mugging, a car crash, a natural disaster. One moment, life is normal. Next, everything has changed.

Chronic Trauma – Pain that doesn't come in one blow but in relentless waves. Domestic violence. Workplace harassment. Bullying. The kind of suffering that doesn't end overnight.

Complex Trauma – A tangled web of trauma often rooted in childhood. It doesn't just affect particular moments, it shapes identities. It's the child who grows up walking on eggshells, only to become an adult who flinches at kindness, expecting it to come with conditions.

Meera grew up in a home where love was unpredictable, where warmth was often followed by cold indifference. Now, as an adult, even when her colleagues genuinely appreciate her work, she brushes it off. "They're just being polite," she tells herself. Trauma has trained her to expect rejection, even when it's not there.

The truth? Trauma isn't just about what happens. It's about how the mind and body respond. How they learn to anticipate, avoid, and protect.

How Trauma Hijacks Expectations

Imagine a child reaching out for comfort, only to be met with silence. Again. And again. Over time, they stop reaching out. Fast forward to adulthood and that same person struggles to believe in genuine connection.

Trauma rewrites expectations. And not in a good way.

<u>The World Feels Unsafe</u> – A person, who has been betrayed by a loved one, by fate, by life itself, may start expecting danger everywhere. Raj, who was bullied in school, now assumes every whisper; every chuckle in a room is about him. He avoids social gatherings altogether, convinced people will always be unkind.

<u>A Self-Fulfilling Prophecy</u> – Repeated failure or rejection can convince someone that good things just aren't for them. Anita grew up with relentless criticism. Now, even in a workplace that values her, she hesitates to take initiative. When praised, she dismisses it, because deep down, she expects failure.

<u>Mistrust Becomes the Default</u> – Trauma survivors often swing between trusting too much (desperate for connection) or trusting no one (expecting betrayal). Ramesh, raised in a home where love was conditional, now finds himself in toxic relationships. He doesn't even realise it, because manipulation feels familiar.

<u>The Obsession with Control</u> – Life has been unpredictable before. Some cope by controlling every detail, believing perfection will shield them from pain. Others, like Arjun, do the opposite, avoiding decisions altogether, convinced that whatever they do or choose will go wrong.

<u>Fear of Abandonment</u> – Those who've faced neglect or loss may cling too tightly, believing love is fleeting. Kavita, raised by emotionally distant parents, now struggles in relationships. She holds on too hard, suffocating people, only to push them away and prove her worst fear true.

And it's not just psychology, its biology. Studies show prolonged trauma reshapes the brain. The amygdala (remember our good old fear centre) overreacts. The hippocampus (Our memory expert) misfires. The prefrontal cortex (the dependable rational thought team) struggles to regain control. It's not "overreacting." It's neuroscience.

Rewriting the Script: Coping and Healing

Here's the good news: the brain can heal. The past doesn't have to play such a significant role in deciding the future. With the right tools, expectations can be rewritten.

Cognitive Reframing – Trauma whispers, "You're unworthy." Reframing says, "You've survived. You're stronger than you know." Priya, who once believed she was unlovable, learned to challenge these thoughts in therapy. Step by step, she rewrote her own story.

Mindfulness & Grounding – Trauma drags people back into past pain or future fear. Grounding techniques, deep breathing, naming objects in a room, focusing on texture or sound, these brings them back to the present . Aditya, who struggled with PTSD, found relief by simply focusing on his breath.

Taking Small Risks – If someone expects failure, they stop trying. The key? Small, safe risks. Reema, terrified of rejection, started by speaking up in small meetings. Slowly, she built confidence. Now? She leads presentations.

Building a Support System – Trauma isolates. Healing happens in connection. Therapy, support groups, and even one reliable friend can be a lifeline. Vikram, once emotionally numb, found strength in a circle of friends who saw him, not just his trauma.

Professional Help – Trauma rewires the brain, but therapy can reprogram it. CBT (Cognitive Behavioural Therapy), a type of psychotherapy that helps people change their thinking and behaviour, EMDR (Eye Movement Desensitization and Reprocessing) is a psychotherapy technique, particularly effective for treating post-traumatic stress disorder (PTSD) and somatic therapy (helps people release damaging, pent-up emotions in their body by using various mind-body techniques) aren't just buzzwords. They're science-backed methods that work. Rahul, plagued by panic attacks, found peace through EMDR.

Rewriting the Narrative – Trauma survivors often define themselves by their pain. But they are more than their past. Identifying strengths, recognising resilience, and seeing their story as one of survival, not just suffering, changes everything. Meera, once paralysed by fear, now embraces her strength.

Trauma Leaves Scars, Not Destinies

Yes, trauma shapes expectations. But expectations can change.

The past may attempt to influence like an echo, but its influence should not be strong enough to dictate the future. With the right tools, support, and mindset, individuals can shift from expecting the worst to believing in something better. Because healing is a choice. One expectation at a time.

COMPLEXES

THE MIND'S SILENT PUPPETEERS

Ever wonder why some people downplay their achievements while others boast about things they never did? Why do some shrink in a group discussion while others dominate every conversation? The answer often lies in a hidden force controlling their thoughts, words, and actions, its psychological complexes.

Coined by Carl Jung, a complex is a cluster of emotions, memories, and perceptions that deeply influence our behaviour, often without us even realising it. Think of it like an invisible puppet master. You think you're in control, but those old wounds, childhood experiences, or deep-seated beliefs are pulling the strings.

From global icons to legendary figures in Indian mythology, history is filled with personalities whose lives were shaped, or shattered by psychological complexes. Some conquered them; others fell prey.

So, let's unpack these complexes, one by one, and see how they shape our lives, with stories from both the world stage and the rich depths of Indian mythology.

1. Inferiority Complex: The "I'm not Good Enough" Syndrome

Alfred Adler, the Austrian psychologist, was the first to define the inferiority complex state, where someone feels inadequate, often in comparison to others. It's like running a race but believing you've already lost before taking the first step.

Charlie Chaplin - From Poverty to Stardom

Before becoming one of the most iconic entertainers in history, Charlie Chaplin grew up in extreme poverty. His father abandoned the family, his mother suffered from mental illness, and he was sent to a workhouse at age seven. For years, he battled an inferiority complex, feeling like an outsider in the world of entertainment. But rather than let it consume him, Chaplin used humour to turn his pain into art. His struggles became the foundation for The Tramp, a character that resonated with millions.

Karna - The Warrior Who Never Felt He Belonged

Karna, one of the most tragic figures in the Indian Epic Mahabharata, was a warrior of unmatched skill, yet he constantly battled an inferiority complex. Born to Princess Kunti but abandoned at birth, raised as a charioteer's son, and denied respect because of his lower social status. Karna spent his entire life trying to prove himself. His deep-seated need for validation made him blindly loyal to Duryodhana, ultimately leading to his downfall.

The Dalit Struggle for Recognition – Dr. B R Ambedkar

For centuries, India's caste system created deep-rooted inferiority complexes. Take Dr. B.R. Ambedkar, born into an "untouchable" caste, he was ridiculed and denied basic rights. But instead of letting inferiority consume him, he used education as his weapon, earned multiple degrees, and became the architect of the Indian Constitution. His life proves that complexes don't define you, your actions does. .

2. Superiority Complex: The "I'm better than Everyone" Illusion

Now, here's the flip side. While inferiority makes people shrink, superiority makes them inflate but the root cause is often the same: insecurity. People with a superiority complex act overly confident, dismiss others, or exaggerate their abilities to mask their self-doubt.

Adolf Hitler-Arrogance Leading to Ruin

Hitler believed in Aryan supremacy and saw himself as a leader destined to reshape the world. His god-like self-perception led him to ignore military advice, launch reckless invasions, and overestimate his army's strength. His unchecked arrogance and refusal to accept reality led to catastrophic failure, proving that a superiority complex can blind even the most powerful.

Ravana - Genius, But Blinded by Arrogance

Ravana, the demon king of another Indian Epic, Ramayana, was an unmatched scholar, a master of the Vedas, and a warrior so powerful that even the gods feared him. But his superiority complex blinded him. He believed he was invincible, which led him to abduct Sita and underestimate Lord Rama. His downfall was not due to a lack of power, but due to his ego-driven overconfidence.

Vijay Mallya and the Illusion of Invincibility

For those unaware about Vijay Mallya, He is an Indian businessman, and former Member of Parliament, known for his liquor empire and the now-defunct Kingfisher Airlines. Once called the “King of Good Times” for his lavish lifestyle, he fled India in 2016 amid allegations of financial fraud and defaulting on loans worth over ₹9,000 crore. He remains in the UK, fighting extradition.

For years, Vijay Mallya lived like a king, with luxury jets, expensive parties, and a business empire that seemed untouchable. But behind the flamboyant image was a financial mess, hidden under an illusion of superiority. When reality caught up, his empire collapsed, and he fled India to escape legal consequences.

3. Guilt Complex: The "I Don't Deserve Happiness" Trap

Ever met someone who constantly blames themselves for everything? Whether it's a failed relationship, a bad business deal, or even something out of their control, they carry guilt like an emotional backpack.

<u>Princess Diana -Trapped in an Emotional Storm</u>

Princess Diana, adored by millions, struggled with guilt throughout her life. Whether it was feeling unworthy of royal status, her troubled marriage, or even the pressure of being a public figure. This self-imposed guilt led to eating disorders and self-destructive tendencies, showing how emotional burdens can consume even the strongest individuals.

<u>Yudhishthira King Who Couldn't Forgive Himself</u>

In the Indian Epic Mahabharata, Yudhishthira was the eldest of the Pandava, known for his unwavering sense of dharma (duty). But his guilt complex haunted him. He blamed himself for the Kurukshetra war, the deaths of his loved ones, and even his mother Kunti's secrets. Despite ruling as a just king, he never truly found peace, showing how guilt can consume even the noblest of men.

4. God Complex: The "I Am Untouchable" Delusion

If superiority complex is an inflated ego, God complex is ego on steroids. It's when someone genuinely believes they are above the rules, incapable of mistakes, and superior to everyone else.

Kanye West: The Creative Genius Who Defied Gravity

Kanye West, the Grammy-winning artist and fashion mogul, is a modern embodiment of the God complex. His unshakable belief in his genius has led to ground-breaking music, innovative fashion lines, and a cultural influence spanning industries. Kanye's confidence has often pushed boundaries, like when he declared himself the "greatest artist of all time" or disrupted award shows to challenge norms. Yet, this same self-assuredness has also led to controversial moments, from public outbursts to polarising statements that alienated fans and critics alike. His story is a reminder that a God complex can drive innovation and self-destruction, both at the same time.

Duryodhana -The Man Who Refused to Bow

Duryodhana, the Kaurava prince in the Mahabharata, believed he was the rightful king of Hastinapur. He dismissed wisdom, ignored good advice, and rejected peace offers, even from Lord Krishna himself! His blind arrogance and refusal to see reason led to the greatest war in history, showing how a God complex can destroy everything.

Breaking Free: How to Unpack These Complexes

We all carry some form of a psychological complex, it is a part of being human. The key is to recognise it before it controls us.

Let's look at some ways to start unpacking these complexes.

Self-awareness: Ask, "Why do I react this way?" or "Is this thought true?"

Challenge the narrative: If you feel inferior, remember that even the best, once doubted themselves. If you feel superior, remind yourself there's always more to learn.

Reframe failures: Instead of "I failed, so I'm worthless", say "I failed, so I learned".

At the end of the day, complexes are just mental luggage. Some bags are heavier than others, but you don't have to carry them forever. So, maybe it's time to unzip that suitcase, let go of what's weighing you down, and start travelling a little lighter. Because the freer your mind, the farther you go.

Recognising and Addressing Personal Complexes: Unmasking the Invisible Chains

Ever walked into a room and felt like you didn't belong? Or maybe you've met someone who talks as if they're the smartest person alive? These aren't just quirks; they might be deep-seated psychological complexes running the show from behind the curtain.

The tricky part? Most people don't even realise they have them. Like a fish that doesn't know it's in water, we swim in our complexes every day. Until someone or something forces us to take a step back.

But here's the good news. Complexes aren't life sentences. The moment you recognise them, you can start breaking free. Let's look at how to spot and address these hidden forces with real-life stories from history, modern India, and even our own lives.

<u>Step 1:</u> Spot the Patterns - What Keeps Repeating?

Complexes aren't onetime events. They show up again and again, like an annoying song stuck on repeat. If you always feel like people are judging you, or if you constantly seek validation, it's time to pause and ask: Why?

J.K. Rowling - From Rejection to Resilience

Before becoming a literary legend, J.K. Rowling faced 12 rejections for Harry Potter. For years, she struggled with self-doubt and felt unworthy of success - a classic sign of an inferiority complex. But instead of letting rejection define her, she started recognising her patterns. She reframed failure as a stepping stone rather than a dead end, and the rest is history.

How do we apply this in our lives?

Write down moments when you feel extremely inadequate or overly superior.

Look for recurring themes, what triggers these emotions?

Recognize that these feelings aren't facts; they're just old stories that your mind keeps telling you.

Step 2: Question the Source - Where Did This Start?

Behind every complex is a story, a childhood incident, a repeated criticism, or even societal conditioning. To break free, you must trace it back to its roots.

Amitabh Bachchan's Career Revival

Amitabh Bachchan is a legendary Indian actor, often called the "Shahenshah (King of Kings) of Bollywood," known for his deep voice, towering presence, and iconic roles spanning over 50 years. He rose to superstardom in the 1970s as the "angry young man" of Indian cinema and remains a cultural icon, hosting Kaun Banega Crorepati (India's Who Wants to Be a Millionaire?). Beyond acting, he's admired for his humility, work ethic, and enduring influence across generations in films, TV, and social causes.

In the late 1990s, Amitabh Bachchan faced massive financial failure. The once-unstoppable superstar was drowning in debt, and his career seemed over. Many in Bollywood wrote him off, reinforcing his fear of irrelevance. But instead of giving in to this self-doubt, he asked himself: Why do I believe I'm finished?

His answer? Because society says ageing actors don't get a second chance. But was that true? No. He reinvented himself with Kaun Banega Crorepati and movies like Mohabbatein, proving that complexes are just mental prisons, if you don't accept the walls, they can't hold you back.

How do we apply this in our lives?

Ask: When did I first feel this way?

Was it a teacher, a parent, or society that planted this idea?

Is this belief true, or just something I accepted without questioning?

Step 3: Challenge the Narrative: Rewriting the Mental Script

Once you identify the source, flip the script. Instead of saying, 'I always fail', try 'I've failed before, but I've also succeeded before'. Instead of 'I need to prove myself', try 'I am enough as I am'.

Ratan Tata-the Rejection That Built an Empire

Ratan Tata is an Indian business legend who transformed the 150-year-old Tata Group into a global powerhouse while championing ethics and innovation. Known for his humility, he led landmark projects like the Tata Nano and Tata Steel, and donated billions to education and healthcare. A role model for leaders, he proves that success and kindness can go hand in hand.

When Ratan Tata tried to expand into the car business with the Tata Indica, it initially flopped. Feeling he had failed the company, he considered selling Tata Motors to Ford. When he visited Ford's headquarters, their executives mocked him, saying they'd be "doing him a favour" by buying it.

That moment could have cemented an inferiority complex, but instead, Tata challenged the narrative. He decided he wasn't a failure, and instead of quitting, he revamped Tata Motors. A few years later, Ford was in crisis, and guess what? Tata bought their Jaguar and Land Rover brands.

How do we apply this in our lives?

When you hear the negative voice in your head, ask: Would I say this to a friend?

Replace self-doubt with self-compassion.

Remember: One failure doesn't define you, what you do next does.

<u>Step 4:</u> Take Small, Bold Actions - Prove Yourself Wrong

Breaking a complex isn't just about thinking differently, it's about acting differently. Once you've recognised the pattern, questioned the source, and rewritten the narrative, the final step is to take action that contradicts your old belief.

P.V. Sindhu - Breaking Barriers in Indian Sports

P.V. Sindhu, India's badminton icon, is a 2-time Olympic medallist and World Champion who redefined women's sports in India with her grit and grace. For decades, Indian sports outside cricket were seen as secondary, especially for women. Many believed Indian women couldn't compete internationally. But P.V. Sindhu refused to accept that narrative. She challenged the deep-seated inferiority complex in Indian sports by winning Olympic silver and gold, proving that India could dominate in badminton.

Her journey wasn't just about talent - it was about taking action despite the doubts and societal conditioning.

How do we apply this in our lives?

If you always feel like you're not good enough, do something you'd normally avoid - apply for that job, speak up in that meeting, start that project.

If you think you always have to be perfect, try doing something imperfectly and be okay with it.

Action rewires belief. The more you challenge your complex, the weaker it gets.

You Are Not Your Complexes

Your complexes are just mental habits, they are not who you are. The key is to spot them, question them, and take actions that prove them wrong.

And here's the kicker, everyone has complexes. Even the most successful people have moments of doubt, arrogance, guilt, or overconfidence. The difference is, they don't let it define them.

So, what's your complex? And more importantly, are you ready to break free?

Overcoming the Impact of Complexes on Expectations: Breaking Free from Mental Roadblocks

Ever felt like you're doomed to fail before even starting? Or maybe you've convinced yourself that if something doesn't go perfectly, it's not worth doing at all?

That's not fate talking. That's your complexes shaping your expectations, and not in a good way.

Complexes, whether they come from childhood conditioning, past failures, or societal norms-warp our expectations. They make us aim too low (because we don't believe we're capable) or set impossible standards (because we fear anything less than perfection is failure). Either way, they keep us trapped.

But here's the thing - expectations aren't facts. They are just stories we tell ourselves. And just like any other story, they can be rewritten.

So let's explore how to break free. With instances from history, Indian legends, and modern era success stories.

<u>Step 1:</u> Recognising the Invisible Chains - Where Do your Expectations Come From?

Think about it. Why do you expect what you expect?

Do you expect failure because you've failed before?

Do you expect perfection because that's what you were taught?

Do you avoid aiming too high because you don't want to be disappointed?

Most of our expectations aren't our own. They come from parents, teachers, society, past experiences- things we never consciously chose. But if you didn't choose them, you can change them.

Dipa Karmakar - Defying India's Gymnastics Expectations

For decades, Indians believed that gymnastics wasn't our thing. It was a sport dominated by countries like the U.S. and Russia, and no Indian had ever qualified for an Olympic final. So what did people expect? Failure.

But Dipa Karmakar refused to accept that. She trained in poor conditions, without world-class facilities, and mastered the "Produnova"- one of the riskiest vaults in gymnastics. Everyone told her not to try it, because "Indians don't do that." But she did it anyway, and became the first Indian woman to reach an Olympic final in gymnastics in 2016.

Key Takeaway: Your expectations are often shaped by what's "normal" around you. Question that "normal." Who says you can't?

Step 2: Breaking the Self-Fulfilling Prophecy - When You Expect Less, You Get Less

Expectations shape reality. If you believe you'll fail, you'll unconsciously make choices that prove yourself right. You won't even try if you believe you're not good enough.

But the reverse is also true: If you expect better, you'll push yourself to achieve better.

Shah Rukh Khan - From an "Ordinary" Boy to the King of Bollywood

Imagine being a middle-class Delhi boy with no godfather in Bollywood. What are the expectations? Maybe you get a few small roles, struggle, and disappear.

But Shah Rukh Khan didn't accept those expectations. He expected to be great, even when no one else did. He once said in an interview, "I always believed I was meant to be the best. Not because I was arrogant, but because I refused to believe otherwise."

His self-belief shaped his choices. He took bold roles, worked like a madman, and rewrote the rules of Bollywood stardom. His expectations shaped his reality.

Key Takeaway: If you set low expectations for yourself, you'll stay small. But if you dare to believe in more, you'll start making choices that align with that belief.

Step 3: Overcoming Fear - The Expectation of Perfection is a Trap

Many people don't struggle with low expectations. They struggle with impossibly high ones. If you expect perfection from yourself, you'll always feel like a failure.

Arjuna's Perfection Obsession vs. Krishna's Lesson

In the Mahabharata, Arjuna the greatest warrior was obsessed with being perfect. He wanted to win every battle flawlessly. But when he saw the battlefield of Kurukshetra, he froze.

Why? Because his expectation of perfection clashed with reality. He wanted a clean, heroic war, but real battles are messy. His fear of failure almost made him quit before the fight even started.

Krishna's advice? "You must act, not to control the results."

Key Takeaway - If you expect that everything must go perfectly, you'll either never start or constantly feel like you're falling short. Focus less on the need to be perfect and more on the progress you make.

Step 4: Challenging "Logical" Expectations - Sometimes, the Impossible is Possible

Sometimes, expectations are based on "logic." We tell ourselves: I'm too old to start over. This has never been done before, so it won't work. I don't have the right background, so I'll never succeed. But what if these "logical" expectations were limiting beliefs?

Ratan Tata and the Nano Dream

When Ratan Tata announced he wanted to make a car for ₹1 lakh (Rupees One Hundred Thousand), people laughed at him. Car manufacturers said it was "impossible" - the cost of materials alone was too high.

But Tata refused to accept "logical" expectations. His team innovated, reduced costs, and created the Nano - the cheapest car in the world.

Did it revolutionise the market? Maybe not. But did it prove that expectations can be shattered? Absolutely.

Key Takeaway: The world will always tell you what's "realistic." But real change happens when you challenge those limits.

Rewrite Your Expectations, Because They Shape Your Future

Look at your life today. Are you aiming lower than you should because you don't believe you can do more?

Are you expecting perfection and feeling miserable when you fall short? Assuming something is "impossible" just because no one around you has done it?

If yes, it's time to rewrite your expectations.

Write down one area where you have low expectations (E.g., "I'll never be good at public speaking.")

Ask: Who gave you this belief? (Did someone criticise you? Did you fail once and never try again?)

Flip the script. (Instead of "I'll never be good," try "I can improve with practice.")

Take one action to prove your new belief. (Sign up for a small speaking event. Take a course. Try once, imperfectly.)

Repeat. Expect More. Act Boldly. Rewrite the Story.

Because at the end of the day, your expectations aren't just thoughts. They are blueprints for your future.

MINDFUL MINDSET

THE KEY TO BUILDING WITHOUT BREAKING

Have you ever driven to a destination, parked your car, and then realised you barely remember the journey? You were physically there, hands on the wheel, eyes on the road-yet mentally, you were somewhere else. That, my friend, is the opposite of mindfulness.

Now, imagine the flip side. What if, instead of being lost in thought, you were truly present, aware of the coolness of the steering wheel, the rhythm of your breath, the sunlight bouncing off the buildings? That's mindfulness in action. And mastering it? That's the gateway to a sharper, calmer, and more intentional life.

Mindfulness: Not Just a Buzzword, But a Superpower

Let's strip away the clichés. Mindfulness isn't just about sitting cross-legged and chanting "Om." It's about training your mind to focus on the now, not the regrets of the past or the anxieties of the future.

Think of your mind as a muscle. Left unattended, it runs wild-chasing thoughts, dwelling on worries, and bouncing from one distraction to another. But when trained? It becomes razor-sharp, filtering out the noise and focusing only on what truly matters.

How to Build a Mindful Mindset?

Developing mindfulness isn't about flipping a switch. It's a process - like sculpting a masterpiece, one careful stroke at a time.

1. Pause, Breathe, Observe
   Ever watched a cat just sitting by the window, gazing at the world? It's not fidgeting, not planning its next move - it's just watching. Try that. Take a pause. Breathe in deeply. Notice your surroundings. You'll be surprised how much of life you've been missing.
2. Tame the Thought Storm
   Your brain is like a monkey, hopping from branch to branch-"What if I fail? What if they don't like me? Did I lock the door?" Instead of getting caught in this thought-induced chaos, just observe your thoughts. Acknowledge them. Let them pass. No need to wrestle with them. Just let them float away, like clouds drifting in the sky.
3. Engage Fully in the Moment

Ever eaten a meal while scrolling your phone, only to realise you don't even remember how it tasted? Try eating mindfully - notice the textures, flavours, and aromas. Do the same for conversations, walks, and even simple moments like washing your hands. Be all in.

4. Detach from Over thinking

   The world's most peaceful minds have one thing in common - they don't over-identify with every thought. You are not your thoughts. They come, they go, and they come again. But they don't define you. Learn to watch them from a distance. Ask yourself: Is this thought helpful (helping me), or harmful (hurting me)? If it's the latter, let it go.

5. Respond, Don't React

   Life throws curveballs. A mindful mindset doesn't mean ignoring problems; it means handling them with clarity. Our natural action is to react impulsively, but that's not what we should be doing. We should hold back, take a breath, assess, and then respond thoughtfully. Your future self will thank you.

The Ultimate Reward: A Mind that's at Peace

Here's the real kicker: when you cultivate mindfulness, life slows down. No! Life doesn't become boring; rather, it becomes interesting in a profound, beautiful way. The noise fades, stress loses its grip, and suddenly, you feel alive. Every moment becomes richer. Even the ordinary ones.

After all, what's the point of rushing through life if you're too distracted to experience it? So, pause. Breathe. Be here. Because the instant present (As of that moment-NOW) is the only moment that truly exists.

Mindfulness: The Secret Weapon for Managing Expectations

Expectations. We all have them. We expect people to understand us. We expect things to go according to plan. We expect life to play fair. And when reality doesn't match up? Disappointment, frustration, even heartbreak.

But what if I told you there's a way to navigate expectations without letting them control you? A way to approach life where you don't constantly feel let down? That's where mindfulness steps in-not just as a feel-good concept, but as a practical tool to keep you sane in an unpredictable world.

Let me use some real-life Scenarios to try and explain how it all works.

<u>The Chocolate Cake Disaster – Learning to Let Go</u>

Meet Priya. She's a perfectionist. So when she decided to bake her best friend a birthday cake, she envisioned a masterpiece - fluffy, moist, pinterest-worthy. She followed the recipe to the letter. But when she pulled her cake out of the oven? A sunken, cracked mess.

I ruined it. I should have been more careful. She'll be so disappointed.

The fallacy (expectation): It must be perfect, or it's a failure.

The reality: Life doesn't care about your expectations.

But here's where mindfulness makes a difference. Instead of ruminating, Priya paused. Took a deep breath. Okay, the cake looks bad, but does it taste good? One bite later, she realised -it's delicious! She decorated it with extra frosting, laughed off the disaster, and guess what? Her friend loved it.

The Lesson? Expectations make you resist reality. Mindfulness helps you accept it. Detach from rigid expectations, and life becomes a lot lighter.

<u>The Promotion That Didn't Happen – Reframing Perspective</u>

Ravi had been working late nights, going the extra mile, waiting for that promotion. And when the announcement came? Someone else got it. The disappointment hit like a truck. Anger, self-doubt, frustration - Was I not good enough?

A mindful person, though, handles such moments differently. Instead of spiralling, Ravi took a step back. He allowed himself to feel the disappointment - mindfulness doesn't mean ignoring emotions, after all. But then he asked:

What can I learn from this? Does this define my worth? What's my next move?

Turns out, the person who got promoted was shifting to a role he wouldn't have even liked. And six months later, Ravi landed a better opportunity elsewhere - one that aligned with his passion.

The Lesson? Disappointments feel crushing when you cling to expectations. But when you step back, breathe, and observe, you realise that setbacks often redirect you to something better.

The "Perfect" Relationship – Seeing Things as They Are

Neha had an image in her mind: the perfect relationship. Romantic dates, constant affection, and reading each other's minds. But the reality? Her partner had different ways of showing love-less grand gestures, quieter presence.

At first, she was frustrated. Why doesn't he do things the way I expect? But then, she practised mindfulness - she observed without judgment. She started noticing the little things: how he made sure she got home safely, how he remembered the small details, how he stood by her through tough times.

The moment she let go of the expectation of love and embraced the experience of love, everything changed.

The Lesson? Mindfulness helps you see reality (things as they are), and not perceived reality (as you wish them to be). And sometimes, that's where the real magic lies.

Bringing It All Together: The Mindful Expectation Shift

We're not saying don't have expectations. We're saying don't be trapped by them.

A mindful mindset teaches you to be flexible. If things don't go as planned, instead of fighting reality, you adapt. It helps you embrace the unexpected. Sometimes, we forget that there could be a possibility that life has better things in store than what we had imagined.

It reminds you that happiness isn't about getting what you dreamed of, but about appreciating what you have got. So, the next time things don't go your way? Pause. Observe. Accept. Adjust.

Because life isn't meant to be controlled, you can't even if you want to. It's meant to be experienced, which you can.

Mindfulness Exercises to Enhance Self-Awareness: A Simple Guide to Knowing Yourself

Ever caught yourself reacting to something before you even realise why? Like snapping at someone and then thinking, Wait… why did I do that? Or feeling restless but not knowing what's bothering you?

That's the thing about self-awareness - it doesn't come automatically. But the good news? You can train your mind to become more aware, just like you train your body at the gym.

And how do you do that? Mindfulness exercises. Think of them as tools - simple, effective, and practical tools that help you understand yourself better. Let's look at some of these exercises.

1. The 5-4-3-2-1 Grounding Exercise – Get Out of Your Head, Into the Moment
   Ever feel overwhelmed, like your mind is on a roller coaster ride that you never wanted to get on in the first place? This is your go-to exercise.
   Pause. Take a deep breath.
   Look around and name:

5 things you can see (the sky, your hands, a book, a shadow, a coffee mug).

4 things you can touch (your shirt, the floor, your chair, your phone).

3 things you can hear (birds chirping, a fan, distant chatter).

2 things you can smell (your perfume, food in the kitchen).

1 thing you can taste (sip water, chew gum, and notice your breath).

Why It Works:

It anchors you in the present moment, cutting through mental noise. The more you practice, the more you'll notice when you're lost in thought, -and that's self-awareness in action.

2. The "Why Am I Feeling This?" Check-In – Understanding Your Emotions

   Ever been in a bad mood but had no clue why? This exercise helps you connect with your emotions before they control you.

   Pause and take a deep breath.

   Ask yourself: What emotions am I feeling right now? Happy? Anxious? Frustrated?

   Now, ask 'why'-gently.

   Example: I'm irritated. → Why? Because my friend didn't reply to my message. → why does that bother me? Because I feel ignored. → Why? Because I value connection.

Don't judge your feelings. Just observe them, like a scientist studying a phenomenon.

Why It Works:

Instead of reacting impulsively, you understand what's driving your emotions. Over time, this makes you more emotionally intelligent and in control of your responses.

3. The "Mirror Talk" – Facing Yourself, Literally

   Want to boost self-awareness and self-acceptance at the same time? Try talking to yourself in the mirror. Sounds weird? Maybe. But it's surprisingly powerful.

   Stand in front of a mirror. Look yourself in the eyes.

   Say: How are you really feeling today?

   Answer honestly, as if talking to a friend.

   If something bothers you, acknowledge it: I feel insecure about my work today.

   Then, reframe: But I'm learning. I'll improve.

   Why It Works:

   Looking at yourself while speaking creates a deeper connection with your inner thoughts, and you can communicate with your subconscious. Plus, seeing your expressions makes you more aware of your emotional state.

4. The "Observer Mode" – Watching Your Thoughts Like a Movie
   Ever noticed how your mind is constantly chatting? "What if this goes wrong? Did I say the right thing? What will they think?" It's exhausting.
   This exercise helps you step back from your thoughts instead of drowning in them.
   Close your eyes. Take a deep breath.
   Imagine a movie being played on a giant screen in front of you about your thoughts.
   Instead of getting sucked in, just watch. Let the thoughts come and go.
   If a thought grabs your attention, label it: Oh, that's an anxious thought. Then let it pass.
   Stay in this observer mode for a few minutes.
   Why It Works:
   It separates you from your thoughts. You start realising, I am not my thoughts. My thoughts are just visitors. And that, my friend, is a game-changer for self-awareness.

5. The "Daily One-Minute Reflection" – A Simple Self-Awareness Habit
   You don't need a whole hour to practice mindfulness. Just a few minutes a day can make a difference.
   At the end of the day, sit quietly for a few minutes.
   Ask yourself:

What emotions did I feel most today?

What moment stood out to me the most?

What's one thing I learned about myself today?

No right or wrong answers. Just observe and move on.

Why It Works:

It builds the habit of self-awareness without overwhelming you. Small daily check-ins lead to big transformations over time.

Final Thoughts: Self-Awareness is Like a Muscle-Train It Daily

These mindfulness exercises are not magic tricks. They won't suddenly make you an enlightened guru overnight. But if you practice them consistently, you'll start noticing a shift:

You'll catch your emotions before they take over.

You'll understand your reactions instead of just acting on impulse.

You'll be more present, more in tune, more…you.

Because in the end, self-awareness isn't about becoming someone new. It's about positively enhancing what and who you already are. So, are you ready to start?

Applying Mindfulness to Daily Challenges: The Art of Staying Sane in a Chaotic World

Life throws curveballs. Some big, some small, but all capable of messing up your mood, focus, and patience. You wake up thinking it's going to be a great day, and by noon, you're already questioning your existence. Sound familiar?

The real challenge isn't avoiding problems - it's handling them without losing your mind. That's where mindfulness comes in. Not as some fancy concept, but as a real, practical tool for tackling everyday struggles.

Let's break it down with three real-life scenarios - personal, professional, and family - where mindfulness can turn frustration into clarity.

1. The 'Why is Everything Going Wrong?' Morning – Personal Life

Imagine this. You wake up late. Your phone's on 5% battery. You spill coffee on your shirt. You rush out, only to realise you left your wallet at home. Now you're stuck at a traffic signal, fuming. Why me? Why today? That's a very normal human reaction. Happens to all of us sometimes or the other. But if we were to convert these reactions using our responses, transformation happens.

Mindless Reaction:

Complain.

Blame the universe.

Flare up at the next person who crosses your path.

Mindful Response:

Pause. Take a deep breath.

Accept: Okay, today's messy. But that doesn't mean I can't still choose how I react. I can!

Reframe: Will this matter in a week? Probably not.

Adjust: Instead of rushing, move with intention. Handle one thing at a time.

Why This Works:

Mindfulness isn't about magically making things better. It's about stopping that mental chain reaction that makes a bad moment turn into a bad day. Pause. Breathe. Reset.

2. The 'Workplace Pressure Cooker' – Professional Life

Meet Arjun. A hardworking guy, but lately, work has been brutal. Emails pile up. Deadlines breathe down his neck. His boss keeps asking for "quick updates" (which, let's be honest, are never quick). Arjun's stress levels? Off the charts.

One day, a co-worker messes up a report that Arjun now has to fix. He's about to explode.

Mindless Reaction:

Snap at the co-worker.

Curse under his breath.

Drown in stress, make more mistakes.

Mindful Response:

Step Back: Arjun notices his clenched jaw, his racing thoughts. He breathes deeply.

Recognise the Pattern: I'm stressed because I feel out of control.

Reframe the Situation: Instead of "Ugh, now I have more work," he thinks, Okay, this is frustrating, but how do I solve it efficiently?

Single-task: He focuses on one thing at a time, finishing faster with less emotional drain.

Why This Works:

Mindfulness doesn't make work easier. No!, But it helps you respond rather than react. It puts you in control of your emotions, so you don't let stress take over.

3. The 'Family Drama Hour' – Home Life

You just sat down to relax. Enter: Family drama. Mom complains you don't call enough. Your spouse seems distant. The kids are fighting over who gets the bigger slice of cake. You can feel your patience evaporating.

Mindless Reaction:

Snap.

Defend.

Walk away, but stay annoyed for hours.

Mindful Response:

Pause before reacting. Instead of jumping in, take a second.

Listen fully. Is Mom upset, or does she just miss me? Is my partner distant, or am I just feeling sensitive today?

Respond calmly. Instead of "Ugh, stop complaining," say, I hear you, Mom. I'll call more. Instead of snapping at your partner, ask Hey, is something on your mind?

For kids? Laugh it off. "How about I take the cake, and you both get broccolis?" Works like magic.

Why This Works:

Family stress often comes from miscommunication, emotional overload, and quick reactions. Mindfulness slows things down, making space for understanding instead of conflict.

Final Takeaway: Mindfulness is a Daily Superpower

It won't stop problems from happening. It will help you navigate them better. Each time you pause, breathe, and choose your response, you break old patterns and build a calmer, stronger, and more self-aware version of yourself.

So next time life throws a tantrum, ask yourself: Do I react? Or do I respond? The choice is yours.

COMMUNICATION AND EXPECTATIONS

THE DANCE OF CLARITY AND CHAOS

Ever played the game of Chinese whispers as a kid? You start with "The cat sat on the mat," and by the time it reaches the tenth person, it somehow morphs into "That fat rat stole my hat!" Funny as a childhood game, but in real life? Miscommunication can be disastrous.

Now, let's take two words that run the world- Communication & Expectations. They are like two dancers in a duet. One misstep, and the whole performance stumbles. The way we communicate determines how expectations are set, met, or shattered.

Scenario 1: The Classic Office Blunder

Imagine this: Your boss sends an email - "Get the report ready ASAP." You, being the diligent employee, burn the midnight oil, crunch numbers, and prepare a detailed 20-page analysis. The next morning, you proudly submit it. What does your boss say?

"I just wanted a one-page summary with key points."

Boom. Expectations vs. reality. The problem? Lack of clarity in communication. Your boss assumed you'd understand what "report" meant, but you interpreted it differently. A simple "Can you prepare a one-page executive summary of the report by 10 AM tomorrow?" could have saved you from a caffeine-fuelled all-nighter.

<u>Scenario 2: Relationships – The Expectation Minefield</u>

Ever heard this? "If you loved me, you would've known!"

Oh boy. Relationships-be it romantic, friendships, or family-are the battlegrounds of unspoken expectations. Your partner might expect flowers on a birthday, but you thought a heartfelt dinner date was more meaningful. Parents might assume you'll call every weekend, while you figured a monthly catch-up was enough.

Here's the kicker: Expectations not communicated become silent disappointments. No one is a mind-reader. Spelling things out, "I'd love it if we could talk at least once a week"-removes the guesswork and the emotional landmines.

<u>Scenario 3: The Customer Service Meltdown</u>

Picture this: You order a "deluxe" room at a fancy hotel, expecting a sea view, a king-sized bed, and some complimentary wine. You walk in and find…a cramped room with a view of the parking lot. You march to the front desk, fuming.

The receptionist? Calm as a monk. "Sir, deluxe just means a bigger bed, not an ocean view."

Ouch. Assumptions strike again. Had the hotel been more specific about what deluxe meant, you wouldn't be standing there contemplating the life choices that led to this moment.

Removing the Gap – The Art of Clear Communication

So, how do we fix this expectation-communication mismatch?

Be Explicit, Not Vague – Instead of saying "soon," say "by 5 PM today." Instead of "Can you handle this?" say "Can you send me a draft by Wednesday?"

Confirm & Clarify – In meetings, instead of assuming everyone understood, ask, "So just to confirm, we're finalising the designs by Friday, correct?"

Manage Expectations Upfront – Before you promise a client "We'll deliver ASAP," define what ASAP means. "We'll take 48 hours to have it delivered."

Check for Assumptions – When you expect something, ask yourself: "Have I communicated this, or am I assuming they'll figure it out?"

The Magic of Over communication

There's a saying: "Bad communication is the father of all misunderstandings." When in doubt, communicate more, not less. The world doesn't need more mind-readers, it needs more clarity. Because when communication is crisp, expectations align, and life? It just flows better.

So, the next time you say something, ask yourself, Did I clearly say what I meant to say? Or am I assuming that they understood what I wanted to say? Because in the great dance of life, getting the steps right will make all the difference.

Strategies for clear and assertive communication

"The single biggest problem in communication is the illusion that it has taken place." - George Bernard Shaw.

Have you ever had a conversation where you thought you were clear, only to later realise that the other person completely misunderstood? Maybe you said, "I need this soon," and they delivered it next week instead of tomorrow. Maybe you asked for "a little help," and they thought you wanted them to take over.

Communication isn't just about speaking - it's about ensuring the message is understood exactly as you intended. And when done right, it has the power to prevent misunderstandings, build strong relationships, and even save you from costly mistakes.

Let's explore eight key strategies for clear and assertive communication, with expanded real-life scenarios to bring them to life.

1. Be Specific: Avoid Vagueness - The $10,000 Mistake
   Raj was a project manager at a fast-growing tech firm. He called a quick meeting with his team and said, "We need this client proposal ready by next week."
   His team assumed "next week" meant Friday, so they planned accordingly. But Raj had meant Monday morning, because the client was expecting it first thing that day.
   On Monday, when the client called asking for the proposal, Raj was caught off guard. The team hadn't even started finalising it yet. Frustrated and embarrassed, he tried to do damage control, but the client was unimpressed and took their business elsewhere - a loss of $10,000 in potential revenue.
   Lesson: Vague instructions leave room for different interpretations. Instead of saying "next week," Raj should have said, "By Monday, 10 AM, I need the final version ready for submission."

Actionable Tip: Always provide exact dates, times, and measurable details. If you say, "Let's meet later," specify "Let's meet at 4 PM."

2. Confirm Understanding with the "Repeat-Back" Method - The Wrong Coffee Order

   Sarah was in a rush at a coffee shop before a big meeting. She ordered, "A caramel macchiato, no sugar, oat milk, extra hot."

   The barista nodded and punched in the order. But when Sarah took the first sip, it was regular milk, with sugar, and barely warm. Annoyed, she walked back to the counter, but by then, she was running late and had no time to get it fixed.

   What went wrong? The barista had misunderstood but never confirmed the details.

   Lesson: Even small misunderstandings can lead to big frustrations. If the barista had repeated back, "So, that's a caramel macchiato, no sugar, oat milk, extra hot?" Sarah could have caught the mistake before it happened.

   Actionable Tip: Always ask the other person to repeat key details back to you. Say, "Just to confirm, what your understanding of what I just asked is?"

3. Use "I" Statements Instead of Blame - The Roommate Conflict

   Emma loved a clean home, but her roommate, Riya, often left dirty dishes in the sink. One evening, after a long day, Emma walked into the kitchen to find a pile of unwashed plates. Frustrated, she stormed into Riya's room and snapped,

"You're so lazy! You never clean up after yourself!"

Riya immediately became defensive. "That's not true! I do clean! Just because I left them today doesn't mean I will never do it!" What started as a minor issue turned into a full-blown argument.

What Could Have Worked Better?

Instead of attacking Riya, Emma could have said,

"I feel frustrated when I see dirty dishes because it makes it hard for me to cook. Could we make a plan to clean up after meals?"

This way, she expressed her feelings without making Riya feel personally attacked.

Actionable Tip: Avoid saying "You always" or "You never." Instead, use "I feel" and focus on the behaviour, not the person.

4. Listen Before You Speak - The CEO Who Transformed His Company

   A company was struggling. Employees felt unheard, morale was low, and resignations were increasing. The CEO, instead of holding another meeting where he just gave a speech, did something different, he called for a town hall and said,

   "Today, I'm not here to talk. I'm here to listen. Tell me what's going wrong."

For 30 minutes, he just listened-no interruptions, no defensiveness.

Employees started opening up. They shared frustrations, concerns, and ideas. By the end of the session, the CEO finally understood what was causing the discontent. Within a few weeks, he implemented real changes based on their feedback, and morale improved dramatically.

Actionable Tip: When someone is speaking, resist the urge to jump in or offer solutions immediately. Instead, say, "What I hear you saying is…" and summarise their point before responding.

5. Set Boundaries and Say "No" When Necessary - The Overworked Employee

Neha was a hardworking graphic designer who always said "yes" to extra work. Her boss would regularly pile on new projects, and Neha, eager to please, never refused.

One day, she found herself juggling five urgent tasks. She was exhausted, stressed, and missed an important deadline. Her boss, instead of appreciating her effort, was furious.

What should Neha have said earlier?

"I'd love to help, but I'm already working on three projects with tight deadlines. Could prioritise, or can someone else assist?"

Actionable Tip: Saying "no" isn't rude-it's necessary. Use polite but firm responses like:
"I don't have the bandwidth for this right now, but I can take it up next week."
"I can do this, but it will delay X. Would that be okay?"

6. Match Your Tone and Body Language to Your Words - The Manager Who Sent Mixed Signals
   A manager called a meeting and told his team, "I'm open to feedback."
   But every time someone spoke, he crossed his arms, frowned, and interrupted. The message was clear, he wasn't open to feedback.
   After a few meetings like this, the team stopped speaking up altogether.
   Actionable Tip: People believe body language more than words. If you want to be approachable, keep an open posture, nod, and maintain calm, even tone.
7. Adapt Your Message to Your Audience - The Jargon Disaster
   A software engineer was presenting updates to the marketing team. He said:
   "We optimised the algorithm by reducing latency and enhancing API throughput."
   The marketing team stared blankly. They had no idea what he meant.
   A better way?

   "We made the app faster, so customers won't experience delays anymore."

   Actionable Tip: Adjust your communication style based on who you're speaking to.

8. Use Analogies and Stories for Clarity - The Doctor Who Explained It Right

   A doctor told a patient, "Your arteries are clogged."

   The patient looked confused. So the doctor tried again:

"Think of your arteries like pipes in a kitchen sink. Over time, grease builds up, and water struggles to flow. We need to clean the pipes before they clog completely."

Suddenly, the patient got it.

Actionable Tip: Use simple analogies to explain complex ideas.

Communication is a Superpower

Great communication isn't about saying more - it's about being understood.

- Be specific.
- Confirm understanding.
- Use "I" statements.
- Listen before responding.
- Set boundaries.
- Match words with body language.

- Adapt to your audience.
- Use analogies for clarity.

Because the best communicators don't just talk - they ensure they're truly heard.

MISUNDERSTANDINGS & CONFLICTS

THE STRUCTURAL WEAKNESS OF ASSUMPTIONS

Conflicts don't always start with shouting matches or dramatic betrayals. More often, they begin quietly, a misheard word, an unanswered message, an assumption that was never clarified.

Imagine this: You wave at a friend across the street. They look in your direction but don't wave back. Your mind immediately spins: Did they ignore me? Are they upset with me? Did I do something wrong? In reality? Maybe they just didn't see you.

Now picture this: You text your friend, "Hey, we need to talk."

In your head, it's just a casual message; maybe you want to discuss weekend plans. But on the other side of the screen, your friend sees it and thinks, "Oh no. What did I do? Is something wrong?"

They start overanalyzing. Did I forget their birthday? Did I say something offensive? By the time you meet, they're defensive, already expecting bad news.

And just like that, a simple message spirals into an unnecessary misunderstanding.

Conflicts and misunderstandings don't always come from big, dramatic events. Most of the time, they creep in from:

- A tone that sounded harsher than intended.
- An assumption that turned out to be false.
- A tiny miscommunication that snowballed.

They happen at work, at home, in friendships, even in text messages, and if left unchecked, they can cause unnecessary frustration, damaged relationships, and even long-term resentment.

That's how misunderstandings work. They are the gaps between what we meant and what was perceived. And if those gaps aren't addressed, they widen into conflicts - some minor, some life-altering.

They happen at work, in friendships, in marriages, even in text messages. But before we learn how to resolve them, we need to understand how they form in the first place.

The Roots of Misunderstandings & Conflicts

1. Assumptions Instead of Clarifications - The Lunch Order Disaster

   Amit was ordering lunch for his office team when his colleague casually said, "Just get me whatever you're getting."

   Amit, a spice-lover, got his favourite fiery curry. But when the food arrived, his colleague stared at the plate, horrified. "You know I can't eat spicy food!" they snapped.

   Amit felt unfairly blamed. "You told me to get you what I was getting!"

   The issue wasn't the food, it was the assumption. The colleague assumed Amit would know their preference. Amit assumed the request was clear.

   Lesson: Assumptions create misunderstandings. A simple clarification- "Get me what you're having, but make sure it's mild"-would have avoided the entire conflict.

2. When Silence Gets Misinterpreted - The Friend Who Thought She Was Ghosted

   Meera sent a text to her best friend, Kavya: "Hey, are we meeting today?"

   Kavya read the message but got distracted and forgot to reply. Hours passed.

Meera, staring at the unread message, fumed. "She's ignoring me? After everything I've done for her?" By the time Kavya finally responded, Meera had built an entire story in her head about being abandoned. In reality? Kavya was just… busy.

Lesson: Don't assume silence means intentional ignorance. Instead of over thinking, just check in: "Hey, just following up! All good?"

3. Clashing Perspectives on Priorities - The Anniversary Dinner Disaster

   Ananya had been looking forward to her anniversary dinner for weeks.

   But as soon as they sat down, her husband, Rohit, picked up his phone. "Just one second," he muttered, replying to work messages. Then another. Then another.

   By the time he looked up, Ananya's mood had soured. "You're always on your phone! You don't even care about tonight!" Rohit snapped back. "It's work! What do you expect me to do?"

   Now, both were angry, but neither was wrong.

   In Ananya's mind: Rohit being on his phone = He doesn't care.

   In Rohit's mind: Responding to work = Being responsible.

Had Rohit just communicated better, "Give me five minutes to wrap this up, then I'm all yours"-the evening would have gone differently.

Lesson: Sometimes, what feels like neglect is just bad timing. Clear communication can bridge that gap.

How to Handle Conflicts When They Happen

1. Pause before Reacting: The 10-Second Rule

   Ever sent an angry text and immediately regretted it? Before reacting in frustration, pause for 10 seconds.

   Ask yourself: Could this be a misunderstanding? Is there a kinder way to interpret this?

   A simple pause can prevent unnecessary fights before they start.

2. Rephrase & Repeat: "So What I Hear You Saying Is…"

   Most conflicts arise because we hear what we assume instead of what was said. Instead of assuming, clarify:

   "So what I hear you saying is, you feel like I've been distant. Is that right?"

   "So you're saying you need help with prioritising tasks, not that you want to drop responsibilities?"

   This small step eliminates assumptions and makes the other person feel heard.

3. Address the Issue, Not the Person - The Roommate War over Dishes

Ankit came home to a sink full of dirty dishes. Annoyed, he turned to his roommate, Sid, and snapped, "You're so lazy! You never clean up after yourself!"

Sid got defensive. "Oh yeah? What about the time you left your laundry lying around for days?" Now, instead of solving the problem, they're attacking each other.

What if Ankit had said, "Hey, can we figure out a system for keeping the sink clean?"

Same frustration. Better communication.

Lesson: Attack the problem, not the person.

4. Ask Instead of Assuming

   Instead of "Why didn't you invite me?" → Ask "Hey, I noticed I wasn't on the invite list, was there a reason?"

   Instead of "You don't care about my opinion." → Ask, "Did my point come across clearly, or do you see it differently?"

   Clarity kills conflict.

5. Find Common Ground Instead of "Winning" - The "You Never Listen" Argument

   Rahul and his wife Priya had been arguing a lot lately. One evening, Priya burst out, "You never listen to me!" Rahul, feeling unfairly accused, retorted, "That's not true! You just keep repeating the same things!"

They were both frustrated, both defensive-neither listening.

Instead, Priya could have said, "I want us to communicate better. How can we make that happen?" Instead of shutting down, Rahul might have responded with a solution, not a counterattack.

Lesson: Instead of fighting to "win," fight to understand.

Communication Fixes More Than It Breaks

Conflicts aren't the problem. The real problem is how we handle them.

- Pause before reacting.
- Clarify before assuming.
- Address the issue, not the person.
- Apologise when needed.
- Pick your battles wisely.

Because at the end of the day, the goal isn't to win arguments - it's to build better relationships. And that? That's always worth the effort.

BUILDING RESILIENCE

THE ART OF BOUNCING BACK LIKE A PRO

Imagine a tightrope walker. High above the ground, balancing on a thin rope, knowing that one misstep could lead to a fall. What keeps them going? Resilience.

Life is that tightrope. Sometimes it's steady. Sometimes the wind howls, the rope sways, and you lose balance. But resilience? That's your safety net. It doesn't mean you won't fall. It means you'll get up after you fall, brush off the dust, and climb back.

Scenario 1: The Tennis Champion Who Refused to Quit

Serena Williams wasn't always the queen of tennis. At 19, she faced a shocking defeat at Wimbledon. Critics said she was done. But instead of breaking down, she broke through-honing her skills, training harder, and coming back to dominate the sport.

Lesson? Resilience isn't about never losing. It's about refusing to be defined by a loss.

Now, ask yourself: When life serves you an ace of problems, do you let it win the match? Or do you return the shot?

Scenario 2: The Business Giant Who Failed His Way to the Top

Ever heard of Colonel Sanders? Before he became the face of KFC, his chicken recipe was rejected 1,009 times. Imagine knocking on a thousand doors and hearing "NO" every single time. Most people would have quit at the tenth rejection. Maybe the hundredth. But 1,009? That's a whole new level of grit.

And yet, on the 1,010th attempt, someone said "YES."

Lesson? Resilience is persistence. It knows that rejection isn't the end. It's just a detour.

Now, ask yourself: How many "no's" have you stopped at? Could the next one be your breakthrough?

Scenario 3: The Student Who Turned Failure Into Strength

Picture a college student named J.K. Rowling-living on welfare, rejected by 12 publishers, and told her book was too "fantasy-driven" to ever sell. Today? Harry Potter has sold over 500 million copies.

Lesson? Resilience believes in yourself, even when the world doesn't.

Now, ask yourself: Do you define yourself by failure? Or by what you do after it?

How Do You Build Resilience?

It's not a magic pill. It's a muscle. You build it every time you refuse to give up.

Reframe failure as feedback. → it's not "I failed." It's "What can I learn?"

Embrace discomfort. → Growth begins where comfort ends.

Develop a "next-play" mentality. → Just like athletes, they don't spend too much o time on the mistake that's just gone, but focus more on the next move.

Find purpose. → People with a why can endure almost anyhow.

Surround yourself with resilient minds. → You raise or fall based on who you surround yourself with.

The Bamboo Secret

Chinese bamboo takes five years to break through the soil. For five years, nothing seems to have happened. But underground, the roots are growing. And when it finally breaks through? It shoots up 90 feet in just six weeks.

Resilience is that underground work. You may not see results today. Or tomorrow. But keep going. Because when the time is right, you'll rise faster than you ever imagined.

So, tell me - are you ready to build your bamboo roots?

Understanding resilience in the context of expectations

Expectations. They shape us, drive us, and sometimes even crush us. Parents expect you to succeed. Society expects you to fit in. You expect life to go a certain way. And when things don't match the script? That's when resilience gets tested.

Resilience isn't just about bouncing back from failures. It's about dealing with the gap between expectations and reality. Let's explore some real-life scenarios to try to understand this better.

Scenario 1: The Perfect Job That Wasn't So Perfect

You ace your interviews, land the job of your dreams, and walk into your first day expecting… what? A team that values you? A boss who appreciates your ideas? Promotions that come with hard work?

Then reality hits. Your ideas are ignored. Your boss micromanages. Your hard work goes unnoticed. The expectation-reality gap hits hard.

What do most people do? Complain. Feel stuck. Maybe quit.

What do resilient people do? Adapt.

Take Satya Nadella. When he joined Microsoft in 1992, it wasn't a glamorous role. The company was rigid, slow, and struggling to innovate. But instead of sulking, he focused on what he could control. He didn't expect instant success. He built his way up, learning, evolving.

Today, He's Microsoft's CEO, leading one of the biggest corporate turnarounds in history.

Lesson - Resilience isn't about wishing that what you expect will happen. It's about reshaping expectations to match reality-then working to make reality better.

Ask yourself - Are you frustrated because reality is unfair? Or because expectations were unrealistic?

Scenario 2: The Love Story That Didn't Go as Planned

Let's talk relationships. You expect your partner to always understand you, always be there, and always align with your dreams. But one day, reality knocks: differences emerge, conflicts arise, and love isn't enough to keep things easy.

Many give up, saying, "This isn't what I signed up for."

But resilient relationships? They shift expectations. They don't seek perfection; they seek growth.

Think of Michelle and Barack Obama. When Barack was deep into politics, Michelle struggled. She felt like a single parent, her expectations of marriage shattered. But instead of walking away, she adjusted, not by lowering standards, but by understanding reality and working through it. They built something stronger than before.

Lesson -Love isn't about finding the perfect person. It's about staying when things aren't perfect and making them better.

Ask yourself - Are you holding onto a fairy-tale expectation, or are you willing to build something real?

<u>Scenario 3: The Dream That Took Longer Than Expected</u>

You set a goal. You expect success in X years. You work, sacrifice, and hustle, only to find yourself nowhere close. Frustration sets in. Why isn't this happening faster?

Enter Sylvester Stallone.

He wanted to be a Hollywood star. Wrote Rocky in three days, believing it would be an instant hit. Expectation? A big paycheck. Reality? 1,500 rejections. At one time, he was so broke that he had to sell his dog to survive. But he didn't let go of resilience. He held on until someone agreed not just to buy the script, but to cast him in the lead.

That persistence turned Rocky into an Oscar-winning classic.

Lesson: Your timeline doesn't control success. Resilience does. Just because something is not happening now doesn't mean it won't happen at all.

Ask yourself - Are you quitting because it's impossible, or just because it's taking longer than expected?

The Core of Resilience: Adjusting, Not Lowering Expectations

Here's where people get resilience wrong. They think it means lowering expectations. It doesn't. It means: Understanding what's in your control and what's not. (You can't control opportunities, but you can control persistence.)

Reframing disappointments as redirections. (Maybe the dream job wasn't right for you, and something better is coming.)

Letting go of the script. (Life is unscripted. The best stories come from unexpected twists.)

The River and the Rock

A rock is stubborn. It expects to stay in one place forever. A river? It doesn't expect anything. It moves, adjusts, and finds another way when blocked. And over time? The river shapes the rock.

Be the river. Adjust, adapt, flow-but never stop moving.

Now, ask yourself: Are your expectations stopping you? Or is it time to adjust and move forward?

Resilience-building exercises and practices: Training Your Mind like an Athlete

Think of resilience like a muscle. You're not born with unshakable strength - you build it. You train for it. You work on it, just like an athlete trains for a marathon or a boxer builds endurance for a fight.

But most people wait until life punches them in the face before thinking about resilience. That's like waiting until race day to start training. Spoiler alert: you won't last.

So, how do you train your mind to be bulletproof? Let's break it down into real-life resilience-building exercises - the mental gym workouts that will prepare you for life's curveballs.

1. The "Control What You Can" Workout - The Job Rejection Spiral
   You apply for your dream job. You craft the perfect résumé, ace the interview… and still get rejected. Ouch. Your brain spirals: Am I not good enough? Should I just give up? Stop! Here's your workout.
   Exercise: The 'Control vs. No Control' List
   Draw two columns.
   On the left, write everything you can't control (e.g., hiring decisions, company politics, the economy).
   On the right, write what you can control (e.g., improving skills, networking, applying elsewhere).
   Now, burn the left side. Seriously. Let it go.
   Lesson: Resilience comes from focusing energy where it makes a difference. The rejection wasn't in your control. Your next move? Concentrate on what you can control.
2. The "Fail Fast, Fail Forward" Drill- The Entrepreneur's Nightmare
   You launch a start-up. You believe in it. But three months in? Sales are dead. Your investor backs out. Everyone tells you to quit. What do you do? You practice failure.
   Exercise: The 'Post-Mortem Success' Technique
   Write down one big failure you've had (business, relationship, project).
   Break it into three key lessons.

Now, create an action plan to apply those lessons in your next attempt.
Example:
Failure: Lost investor.
Lesson: Didn't validate market demand early enough.
Action Plan: Interview 50 potential customers before launching the next idea.
Lesson: Resilience isn't avoiding failure. It's failing better each time.

3. <u>The "Discomfort Training" Routine -</u> The Tough Conversation You Keep Avoiding
   You need to confront your boss, end a toxic relationship, or set a boundary with a friend. But confrontation feels like walking into a fire pit.
   Exercise: The '30-Second Discomfort Challenge'
   Pick something uncomfortable but not dangerous.
   Speak up in a meeting.
   Ask for a discount at a store.
   Start a conversation with a stranger.
   Do it for 30 seconds.
   The goal? Get used to discomfort.
   Lesson: If you can handle small discomforts, you'll be ready for the big ones-like life-changing conversations, career shifts, or standing up for yourself.
4. <u>The "Reframe the Pain" Workout -</u> The Breakup That Feels Like the End

You thought it was forever. You planned your future together. And now? It's over. You feel shattered.

Exercise: The 'Movie Director Method'

Imagine your life is a movie.

You are the director, not just the actor.

Ask: If this were a comeback story, what would the next scene be?

Example:

Scene 1: Heartbreak. Crying. Netflix marathons.

Scene 2: Travel solo. Start a new project.

Scene 3: Meet someone new - or better, become the best version of yourself.

Lesson: Resilience isn't about avoiding pain. It's about deciding what happens next.

5. The "Future You" Visualisation Drill - Feeling Stuck and Lost in Life

   You're overwhelmed. No direction. Every day feels like a loop.

   Exercise: The 'Meet Your Future Self' Practice

   Close your eyes. Imagine yourself five years from now.

   What does future-you look like? Confident? Healthy? Successful?

   Write down three things the future you did to get there.

   Start doing them.

   Example:

   Future-me is fit → Starts working out.

Future-me runs a business → Starts learning finance.
Future-me is confident → Practices public speaking.
Lesson: Resilience is built when you become the person your future self will be proud of and will thank you for becoming.

6. <u>The "Hardship Gratitude" Habit -</u> The "Why Me?" Phase

   Something terrible happens. A loss. A failure. You ask, Why? Why does this keep happening to me? Why only to me?

   Exercise: The 'Find the Hidden Gift' Practice

   For every hardship, force yourself to find a positive outcome.

   Example:

   Lost a job? → Built a side hustle.
   Got rejected? → Dodged the wrong path.
   Heartbreak? → Found independence.

   Lesson: Resilience is realising that even pain has a purpose.

7. <u>The "Resilience Role Model" Method–</u>

   Feeling like no one understands your Struggles. You're stuck. Alone. You think no one else has ever gone through this.

   Exercise: Find a Role Model Who Overcame Something Worse

   Research someone who faced something worse than you and overcame it.

Study how they did it.

Apply their lessons to your own life.

Example:

You feel like giving up? → Read about Thomas Edison failing 10,000 times.

You're struggling financially? → Oprah was once dirt-poor.

You feel like an outcast? → Einstein was expelled from school.

Lesson: Resilience isn't just learned from personal struggle - it's borrowed from others who've been there.

Final Thought: The Samurai Mindset

In ancient Japan, samurai trained their minds as much as their swords. They didn't wait for battle to build strength. They trained every day, so when the moment came, they were ready.

Life will test you. That's a given. But will you be ready?

Resilience isn't a personality trait. It's a practice. And just like any workout, the more you do it, the stronger you become.

Now, the question is, which exercise are you starting today?

CULTIVATING A POSITIVE MINDSET

A REAL-WORLD TRAINING GUIDE

Let's get one thing straight: positivity is not naivety.

It's not about pretending everything is sunshine and rainbows when life is throwing thunderstorms. It's not about suppressing pain or faking smiles. It's about training your mind to find opportunity in adversity, clarity in chaos, and strength in struggle.

Positivity is a skill. And like any skill, it can be built on, improved, and eventually mastered.

So, how do we cultivate a positive mindset? Through training. Let's dive into real-life exercises that will rewire your thinking, so that no matter what life throws at you, you see the possibilities instead of the problems.

1. <u>The "Morning Mindset Reset" Exercise -</u> The "Dreaded Alarm Clock" Syndrome
   You wake up. First thought? Ugh, another day. Your brain instantly downloads a mental list of worries: deadlines, stress, unfinished work, responsibilities.

Your day starts with negativity before you even leave your bed.

We fix this by doing the "3 Powerful Questions" Practice

Before you touch your phone, ask yourself:

What am I excited about today? (Even something small - coffee, a workout, a favourite song.)

What is one thing I can do to make today better? (A smile, a compliment, a deep breath before reacting.)

What am I grateful for right now? (Health, family, opportunities, and lessons learned.)

What's happening? Your brain is being forced to search for the good instead of defaulting to stress. Over time, this becomes your default setting.

2. The "Mental Diet" Practice - The Doom Scrolling Habit

   It's 10 PM. You pick up your phone to check a notification. Two hours later, you're drowning in bad news, comparing your life to strangers on Instagram, and somehow ended up reading about an economic crisis in a country you've never been to.

   And now? You feel drained, anxious, and demotivated.

   To avoid this situation, you need to take the "Mindful Consumption Challenge."

   Audit your inputs. What are you feeding your mind? Social media? News? Gossip?

   Replace one negative input with a positive one.

Swap 15 minutes of doom scrolling for an inspiring podcast.

Replace sensational news with books that expand your perspective.

Unfollow negativity, follow motivation.

Why does this work? Your mindset is created and crafted by what you consume. Garbage in, garbage out. But if you keep feeding your mind empowering, motivating, feel-happy content, positivity becomes your natural state.

3. The "Reframe the Challenge" Drill - The "Why Me?" Mindset

   Your boss gives you a crushing workload. A project fails. A relationship ends. Your first thought? Why does this always happen to me? Negativity thrives in a victim mentality. But resilient people, they reframe. For that, you need to follow the "Game Plan Shift" Method

   When faced with a challenge, ask:

   What is this teaching me? (Growth, patience, better decision-making?)

   How can I turn this into an advantage? (A setback that forces reinvention?)

   What would the strongest version of me do?

   Example:

   Lost a job? → Now's the chance to build that side hustle.

Breakup? → Time to focus on self and become better, unshakable.

Failure? → A redirection, not a rejection.

Why does this work? Your brain moves from victim to strategist. Instead of reacting emotionally, you respond with power.

4. <u>The "Reverse Gratitude" Exercise:</u> Taking Things for Granted

   You have a roof over your head. Food on your plate. People who care about you. But you rarely feel grateful until something is gone. Try the "What If It Wasn't There?" Challenge.

   Pick three things you take for granted (your job, health, family, even Wi-Fi).

   Imagine waking up tomorrow and they're gone.

   Sit with that thought for a minute.

   Now, appreciate them as if you just got them back.

   Example:

   What if today were the last day you could walk? Suddenly, every step feels like a gift.

   What if your Wi-Fi crashed forever? That ordinary connection now seems magical.

   Why does this work? Your brain stops chasing happiness in the future and starts feeling it in the present.

5. <u>The "Break the Negativity Loop" Challenge -</u> The Bad Day Spiral

One bad thing happens in the morning: traffic, spilt coffee, and an annoying email. Your brain decides: Great, today is ruined. Negativity snowballs if unchecked. Here's how to stop it. Use the "Reset Ritual"

When something bad happens, interrupt the cycle.

Physically shift-go for a walk, splash cold water on your face, listen to an upbeat song.

Say out loud: "This moment does not define my day."

Example:

Your meeting went horribly? Doesn't mean the whole day is ruined.

A friend cancels plans? Doesn't mean no one cares.

Why does this work? It teaches your brain that one bad moment ≠ bad day. You reclaim control.

6. <u>The "Small Wins" Tracker -</u> Feeling Like You Are Not Making Progress

   You set big goals but feel stuck. The finish line always seems far away, the distance left to the finish line never seems to reduce, and hence, your motivation drops. Maintain the "Daily Victory Log"

   At the end of each day, write down three wins. Big or small. Anything counts.

   Example:

   Sent that email you were procrastinating on?

   Choose a healthy meal instead of junk?

   Didn't lose your temper in traffic?

Why does this work? Your brain builds momentum. Instead of focusing on what's wrong or not, you celebrate what's there and what's working. And small wins? They add up.

7. <u>The "Future You" Visualisation -</u> Doubting Your Potential
   You see others winning, succeeding, thriving and you wonder, Can I ever get there? Imbibe the "Meet Your Future Self" Practice

Close your eyes. Now see yourself 5 years from now. What do you see? Do you see yourself in an improved version or the same? Are you Confident? Successful? Strong?

What daily habits got them there? Start doing them now.

Example:

Future-you is fit? → Exercise today.

Future-you is financially free? → Learn investing today.

Future-you is happy? → Start choosing joy today.

Why does this work? It shifts your mind from "I hope I succeed" to "I am becoming that person now."

<u>Final Thought: The Farmer's Secret</u>

A farmer plants seeds. He waters them. He nurtures them. For weeks, there's been nothing visible. Then, suddenly, growth.

A positive mindset is built the same way. Daily training, daily planting, daily nurturing. One day, without even realising how it happened, you will wake up and, voila! You have developed the positive mindset that you have been working on. Just like that!

So, the real question is: Which seed will you plant today?

THE ART OF EXPECTATION MANAGEMENT

10 REAL-LIFE SUCCESS STORIES

Expectation is everything!

Think about it. A good meal tastes better when you weren't expecting much. A movie feels disappointing if the hype is sky-high. A team winning a championship feels historic when no one saw it coming, but just "business as usual" when it's a favourite.

Expectation shapes reality. It frames how we perceive success, failure, and everything in between.

That's why the most successful companies, leaders, and innovators don't just deliver results. They design expectations so that when the results arrive, they feel even more powerful.

How do they do it? How do some businesses keep customers thrilled, some leaders turn crises into comebacks, and some brands keep us hooked year after year?

Let's take a deep dive into 10 real-world cases of masterful expectation management - from Apple to Amazon, Disney to the Olympics, and even a life or death space mission.

Get ready, because once you see how it works, you'll never look at success the same way again.

1. **Steve Jobs and the iPhone Launch:** Under promise, Over deliver

   Imagine telling the world in 2006 that a phone could play music, browse the internet, and fit into your pocket seamlessly. You'd have been laughed out of the room. But Steve Jobs? He carefully managed expectations.

   Challenge:

   The mobile phone market was already crowded with dominant players like Nokia, BlackBerry, and Motorola.

   People were sceptical - could a company that made computers revolutionise phones?

   Overpromising could have led to backlash if the product had flaws.

   Resolution:

   Jobs kept the messaging simple but ambitious. He didn't call it the best phone, just a combination of an iPod, a phone, and an internet communicator.

Apple focused on experience over specs, making sure that people felt the difference once they used it. The first iPhone wasn't perfect, but because expectations were managed well, people were delighted rather than disappointed.

When he introduced the iPhone in 2007, he didn't market it as just a new phone. He called it "an iPod, a phone, and an internet communicator." That was it! Simple, clear, but revolutionary.

Expectation management here was masterful. By keeping the promise broad but not overreaching, Apple created excitement without the risk of underwhelming. When people finally got their hands on it, it wasn't just a gadget, it was magic.

Lesson: Under promise, over deliver, and let the experience speak for itself.

2. **Disney Theme Parks:** The Power of "Waiting Time" Psychology

   You're at Disneyland, and the board says, "Estimated wait time: 60 minutes."

   You sigh, brace yourself… and get on the ride in 45 minutes. Relief!

   Challenge:

   Long wait times can make customers frustrated and ruin their experience.

If guests feel misled about waiting times, trust in Disney's operations would decline.

Park visitors need a sense of control over their time.

Resolution:

Disney intentionally inflates wait time estimates, so people feel relief when they get on the ride sooner than expected.

They implemented FastPass and Genie+ systems to give visitors an option to control their queue experience.

Entertainment in the queue areas (screens, music, character appearances) ensures that waiting doesn't feel as painful.

Disney doesn't just manage expectations, they design them. By slightly inflating wait times, they ensure people feel pleasantly surprised. If the board had said 30 minutes and it took 45, frustration would have crept in.

It's a small psychological trick, but a massive win in customer satisfaction.

Lesson: People don't get upset because they wait. They get upset when they wait longer than they expected. Managing perceived expectations is more powerful than reducing actual wait times.

3. **Amazon Prime:** Setting Speed as the Expectation

   A decade ago, fast delivery meant 5-7 business days. Then Amazon came along and said, "Two days or less." It rewired people's minds.

   Challenge:

   Consumers were used to 5-7 business days as standard shipping time.

   If Amazon promised too fast a delivery and failed, it would damage trust.

   They had to scale logistics while keeping fulfilment centres cost-efficient.

   Resolution:

   Instead of promising overnight delivery to everyone, Amazon set a two-day benchmark, which felt fast but was feasible.

   The company built infrastructure first (warehouses, AI-driven logistics) before making aggressive speed claims. Surprise early deliveries made customers feel like they got extra value.

   But here's the genius part: Amazon didn't just promise fast shipping - they created a system where their fastest deliveries were often even faster than advertised. When your package arrives in one day instead of two, it feels like a gift.

   Meanwhile, competitors who promised "3-day shipping" but took 4 days? Disappointment.

Lesson: If you can control the benchmark, you control the perception. Amazon made fast the new normal, and now, anything slower feels unacceptable.

4. **Tesla's Autopilot:** Managing Hype (Almost Failing at It)

   Tesla's Autopilot feature was game-changing. But when Elon Musk called it "Full Self-Driving," people expected… well, an actual driverless car.

   Challenge:

   "Full Self-Driving" set an expectation that cars could drive themselves, which wasn't entirely true.

   High-profile accidents involving Tesla's Autopilot created a perception problem.

   Customers who misunderstood the technology expected zero human intervention.

   Resolution:

   Tesla rebranded the feature and now focuses more on driver assistance rather than autonomy.

   They added disclaimers and safety reminders to reinforce that drivers must remain alert.

   The company pivoted its messaging from "self-driving" to "the best driver assistance system in the world."

   Reality? It still requires human supervision. The expectation gap led to lawsuits, criticism, and public scepticism.

But here's how Tesla pivoted:

They rebranded the feature while keeping the same tech.

They now emphasise "driver assistance" rather than "self-driving."

The damage control worked, and people adjusted their expectations.

Lesson: If you overpromise, you will have to recalibrate expectations later and that's harder than setting the right ones upfront.

5. **The Apollo 13 Mission:** Expectation Management in a Crisis

   "Houston, we have a problem."

   April 1970. An oxygen tank explodes on Apollo 13. Suddenly, the moon mission turns into a fight for survival.

   Challenge:

   The explosion onboard meant the moon mission was no longer possible.

   Public perception: Would NASA fail on a global stage?

   The astronauts needed psychological stability to ensure survival.

   Resolution:

   NASA did not focus on failure, they quickly shifted the goal from "landing on the moon" to "getting everyone home safely."

Instead of overwhelming astronauts with worst-case scenarios, NASA gave them small, clear tasks to focus on.

Public relations messaging stayed calm, controlled, and solution-oriented, preventing panic.

Here's where NASA's expectation management became legendary: They never said "we might not make it." Instead, they kept the message: "We are figuring it out."

They gave small, achievable goals to the astronauts: "Conserve power, fix the CO2 levels, and prepare for re-entry."

By breaking a crisis into manageable steps, they ensured focus instead of panic. The crew made it back alive.

Lesson: In crises, controlling emotional expectations is as important as solving the problem itself. Calm leadership makes survival possible. Expectation management is about shifting focus from what's lost to what can still be achieved.

6. **Netflix's Binge-Worthy Algorithm:** Managing Content Expectations

   Remember when TV shows had weekly releases? Then Netflix changed the game with "binge-watching."

   But here's the trick: Not all shows drop all at once anymore. Shows like Stranger Things or Money Heist are now released in parts, keeping anticipation high.

Challenge:

If Netflix always released full seasons at once, audiences would consume too quickly and cancel subscriptions.

If they forced weekly releases, customers might get frustrated.

Balancing instant gratification with sustained engagement was key.

Resolution:

They studied user behaviour and started experimenting with split releases (Part 1, Part 2).

Certain high-profile shows still have weekly releases to keep hope alive (The Last Dance, Stranger Things).

Netflix trained audiences to expect different release patterns, reducing backlash.

They've managed viewer expectations by:

Training audiences to expect "Part 1" and "Part 2" instead of "all episodes now."

Using data to decide which series get weekly releases vs. all-at-once drops.

Lesson: Managing expectations isn't about giving people what they want immediately. It's about controlling how and when they experience it. Expectation management isn't about immediate gratification, it's about pacing excitement.

7. **Zara's "Limited Stock" Strategy:** Scarcity as Expectation Control

   Ever walked into a Zara store, found a jacket you loved, and thought, "I'll buy it next time"?

   Next time comes… and it's gone. That's not bad inventory planning. It's an expectation design.

   Challenge:

   If Zara followed a traditional fashion model (stocking items for months), shopping urgency would be low. If they created too much scarcity, customers might get frustrated.

   Resolution:

   Zara trained consumers to expect fast-moving inventory.

   They made shopping feel like a race, reinforcing that if you see something you love, buy it now.

   Limited restocks ensured the scarcity strategy worked without feeling manipulative.

   Zara trains shoppers to expect fast-moving collections. Unlike other brands, they don't restock most items. This forces immediate purchases, because you don't expect it to be there later.

   Lesson: Scarcity isn't just a supply issue. It's an expectation strategy.

8. **Toyota's "Kaizen" Culture:** Expectation of Constant Improvement

Toyota doesn't sell perfection. They sell continuous improvement.

Challenge:

If Toyota marketed its cars as perfect, any flaw would destroy credibility.

They needed a way to build trust while acknowledging limitations.

Resolution:

Toyota introduced Kaizen (continuous improvement) as its brand philosophy.

Instead of promising the best cars today, they promised to always improve, making customers feel part of an evolving experience.

Customers came to expect better versions over time, keeping long-term loyalty high.

Their legendary Kaizen philosophy means they set an expectation: "Our cars aren't flawless today. But tomorrow, they'll be even better."

By openly embracing progress over perfection, they never overpromise and rarely under deliver.

Lesson: If you make improvement part of your brand, expectations will always be positive and evolving. Set expectations that evolve with your product, so people stay with you for the journey.

9. **Google Search:** The Illusion of Instant Answers

   Google shows results before you finish typing. That's expectation engineering.

Challenge:

People want search results instantly, but some queries take time.

If Google promised "instant search" but took 2 seconds, users would feel let down.

Resolution:

Google implemented instant search previews to make results feel faster than they are. Even if the actual search takes 1-2 seconds, that split-second preview makes you feel like it's instant.

Snippet boxes and "People also ask" create an illusion of instant answers.

They show "People also ask" and snippets to make it seem like answers are already there.

They focused on perceived speed rather than actual speed.

Lesson: Speed isn't just about technology. It's about perceived speed. Expectation isn't about reality, it's always about perceived reality!

10. **Olympics & World Cup:** Expectation as Hype Control

    Challenge:

    If these events happened too often, they would lose their magic. If they were too rare, people might lose interest.

    Resolution:

A 4-year cycle ensures anticipation builds naturally. Qualification rounds, marketing campaigns, and countdowns sustain excitement between events. Viewership remains massive because people have waited long enough to care.
By happening once every four years, these events create built-in anticipation. If they happened yearly, they'd lose their magic.
Lesson: Sometimes, the best way to manage expectations is to make people wait.

Final Thought: Expectation is Reality. Expectation Management is the Ultimate Power Move

From tech giants to space missions, entertainment to psychology, every successful venture carefully crafts how people expect an experience.

Whether you're leading a company, managing a team, or even handling personal relationships, one rule holds: Manage expectations right, and you don't just meet them, you exceed them. And that's where true success lies.

Expectation isn't about what's real. It's about what feels real. Master that, and you master success.

REFRAMING

THE ART OF CHANGING THE PICTURE WITHOUT CHANGING THE REALITY

Ever tried looking through a camera lens and shifting the angle just a little? The scene remains the same, but suddenly, the picture feels entirely different. That's reframing the mental equivalent of tilting the lens.

We all have moments when life hands us what seems like a raw deal. A project fails. A promotion slips away. A relationship ends. The immediate reaction? Frustration. Anger. Maybe even self-doubt. But what if, instead of staring at the problem through a narrow, defeatist frame, we shifted the perspective?

Scenario 1: The 'Missed Promotion' or the 'Lucky Escape'?

Imagine you've been eyeing a promotion for months. You put in extra hours, sacrificed weekends, and believed you were a shoo-in. But then-boom! Someone else gets it. The first instinct? This is unfair. I deserved it.

But let's reframe.

What if this so-called setback is a blessing?

What if that role had drained you with stress, leaving you no time for things that truly matter?

What if this rejection is just a nudge toward an even better opportunity?

History is full of reframing stories. Steve Jobs was fired from Apple, the company he built. Devastated? Yes. But years later, he called it "the best thing that could have ever happened to me." Why? Because it forced him to innovate, and that led to Pixar, NeXT, and an even greater Apple comeback.

Scenario 2: The 'Rain Ruined My Plans' or 'A Chance to Pause'?

You've planned a grand picnic with friends, but the skies decide otherwise. It starts pouring. The old frame? Ugh, what a disaster. But wait, what if the rain is a gift?

Maybe it's an invitation to a cosy indoor game night, full of laughter and chai.

Maybe it's a reminder to slow down, curl up with that book you've been neglecting.

Maybe, just maybe, it's nature's way of forcing you to find joy beyond perfect weather.

Scenario 3: 'I'm Not Good at This' or 'I'm Still Learning'?

A child struggles with math. Every wrong answer reinforces the belief-"I'm just not a numbers person." But reframing can shift the entire mindset: "I may not get it yet, but every mistake is one step closer to understanding."

This isn't just motivational fluff. Carol Dweck's research on 'growth mindset' proves that the way we frame failure determines whether we grow or stagnate. The greatest athletes, scientists, and innovators don't see setbacks as stop signs-they see them as stepping stones.

The Power of the Frame

Life throws curveballs. You can either see them as unfair tricks or unexpected detours toward something better. The event itself doesn't change, but the way you interpret it does.

So next time you're caught in a tough spot, ask yourself: Is this a dead end, or just a bend in the road? Maybe all you need is a new frame.

The Reframing Workout: Train Your Mind like a Champion

Want to master the art of reframing? It's not just a mindset shift-it's a muscle. And like any muscle, it needs exercise. You wouldn't expect six-pack abs after one gym session, right? The same goes for mental strength. So here's a practical, no-nonsense Reframing Workout step-by-step exercise routine to rewire your brain for a fresh perspective on life's challenges.

Warm-up: Catch the Frame

Before we change the frame, we need to recognise it. The easiest way to do that is to always carry a small notebook (or use your phone). Every time you feel frustrated, angry, or stuck, write down:

What happened? How do you feel about it? What story are you telling yourself?

Real-Life Example:

Let's say you're stuck in traffic, running late for an important meeting. Your first thought: This is ruining my day! Write that down. Because awareness is the first step to change.

<u>Set 1: Flip the Frame (Reframing Basics)</u>

Now that you've caught the negative frame, let's flip it.

For each negative thought, challenge yourself to find two alternative perspectives.

Real-Life Example:

Situation: Your boss gives tough feedback on your presentation.

Old Frame: I'm terrible at this. I embarrassed myself.

New Frames:

This is free coaching! Now I know exactly what to improve. If my boss is pushing me, it means they see potential in me.

This isn't about toxic positivity. It's about seeing options where you once saw only obstacles.

Set 2: The "What Else?" Challenge

Your brain loves shortcuts. It takes one bad moment and paints the whole situation as terrible. We're about to break that habit.

Every time you catch a negative thought, ask yourself: What else could be true?

Real-Life Example:

Situation: A friend cancels plans last minute.

Old Frame: They don't value our friendship.

New Frames:

Maybe they're going through something and need space.

I suddenly have free time, how can I make the most of it?

Repeat this challenge 5 times a day with different situations. You'll be surprised how many interpretations exist for the same event.

Set 3: The "Story Rewrite" Exercise

We all have memories from our past that continue to affect us, that still hurt. What if we rewrote the story?

Pick one bad memory that still bothers you. Write down the original version of the story (the painful one).

Now, rewrite it with a positive or growth-oriented frame.

Real-Life Example:

Old Story: I failed my start-up. I lost money and wasted time.

New Story: I learned more in two years of running a business than I ever could in an MBA. Now, I'm smarter, tougher, and ready for my next big move.

This isn't about lying to yourself. It's about choosing a version of the truth that serves you instead of trapping you.

Cool Down: Gratitude Reframing

To make reframing second nature, end each day with a Gratitude Reframe. Before bed, write down:

One challenge you faced today.

One hidden benefit that came from it

Example:

Challenge: Had a terrible day at work, felt engulfed in negativity, and felt bad.

Reframe: This showed me I need a better work-life balance-time to set boundaries.

Final Thoughts: The Reframing Muscle Never Stops Growing

Do this workout daily, and soon, reframing won't be something you try-it'll be something you are. The world won't change, but the way you see it will. And sometimes, that makes all the difference.

SELF-REFLECTION WORKSHEET SERIES

Why Reflect? Ever caught yourself staring at the ceiling at 2 AM, questioning your life choices? Good. That means you're human. But instead of letting those thoughts spiral into existential dread, let's channel them into something productive-self-reflection. These worksheets are designed to help you understand yourself better, make wiser decisions, and live a regret-free life. Ready? Let's dive in.

THE MIRROR TEST – Understanding Your True Self

Why it matters - If you don't know who you are, how can you expect to live a life that's truly yours?

Instructions:

Stand in front of a mirror (yes, literally).

Look yourself in the eyes and ask: Who am I?

Now, grab a notebook and answer these questions:

What are my core values? (Hint: Think about what truly angers or excites you.)

What do I love doing even when no one is watching?

What do I pretend to like but secretly dislike?

If money and social pressure didn't exist, what would I be doing?

Write down any patterns you notice.

Closing Thought: If your actions and values don't align, it's time to recalibrate.

THE 80-YEAR-OLD YOU – Making Decisions That Truly Matter

Why it matters - Decisions feel overwhelming until you fast forward time.

Instructions:

Picture yourself at 80 years old, sitting in a rocking chair.

Answer these questions:

Looking back, what do I wish I had done more of?

What do I wish I had worried less about?

What kind of relationships do I want to have maintained?

What stories do I want to be able to tell my grandchildren?

Compare these answers with your current priorities. Are they aligned?

Closing Thought: If your 80-year-old self would cringe at your choices today, it's time to change something.

THE COMFORT ZONE MAP – Identifying Growth Areas

Why it matters - Growth doesn't happen in the comfort zone. But neither does survival in constant panic.

Instructions:

Draw three circles on a page:

Inner Circle: Things I'm 100% comfortable with.

Middle Circle: Things that make me slightly uneasy, but I can manage.

Outer Circle: Things that terrify me but could help me grow.

Fill each circle with examples from your life (e.g., public speaking, asking for a raise, saying no, starting a business).

Pick one from the middle circle and take a small step toward it this week.

Closing Thought: Fear signals potential. Always remember, only if something challenges you, it has the potential to change you.

YOUR LIFE DASHBOARD – Evaluating Different Aspects Of Life

Why it matters - If your life were a car, you wouldn't drive it with a broken engine and flat tires, would you?

Instructions:

Rate the following on a scale of 1-10 (1 = terrible, 10 = thriving):

Health

Relationships

Career

Finances

Mental well-being

Fun & Creativity

Identify the lowest-scoring area and answer:

What's one small action I can take to improve this today?

What's holding me back from doing that?

Commit to one action this week.

Closing Thought: You can't fix everything at once, but you have to start somewhere.

THE ENERGY AUDIT – Finding Out What Drains & Fuels You

Why it matters - You wouldn't pour water into a leaky bucket. So why do it with your energy?

Instructions:

Make two columns: Energisers and Drainers.

Under Energisers, list things that make you feel alive (e.g., certain people, activities, hobbies, routines).

Under Drainers, list things that exhaust you (e.g., toxic conversations, mindless scrolling, tasks you hate).

Identify at least one drainer to reduce and one energiser to increase.

Closing Thought: Energy is your most valuable currency. Spend it wisely.

<u>THE REGRET-FREE LIVING PLAN –</u> Aligning Actions with Values

Why it matters- Regrets are just unexecuted decisions waiting to haunt you.

Instructions:

Write down 3 things you'd regret not doing if life ended tomorrow.

Ask: Why haven't I done them yet?

What's the worst that could happen if I tried?

What's one step I can take this week to move toward them?

Pick one and schedule an action step today.

Closing Thought: A fulfilled life is built on bold steps, not postponed dreams.

Final Challenge: Make Reflection a Habit

Pick one worksheet to complete each week for the next six weeks. Self-awareness isn't a one-time exercise, it's a lifelong habit you need to inculcate into your life.

And remember, your future improved self is watching. Don't let them down.

Happy reflecting!

THE GOAL-SETTING WORKOUT

Sculpting your dreams needs as much discipline as sculpting your body, and they are as important, if not more. They form a major part of your mental wellness, and are primary reasons for negative emotions like depression, anger, frustration and unhappiness.

The Movie Trailer Exercise - If your life were a blockbuster movie, what would the trailer look like?

Instructions:

Imagine a future version of yourself, five years from today. You have achieved everything you ever wanted. Now, visualise it as if you're watching a 90-second movie trailer.

What scenes would play?

What would the voiceover say?

What emotions would it evoke?

Write down the key highlights of this 'trailer' in bullet points. Be specific! Example:

"A standing ovation after my TED Talk on leadership."

"Waking up in my dream house, overlooking the sea."

"Holding the first copy of my published book."

Now, break it down into smaller goals.

What major milestones must be fulfilled or reached to be able to make that scene true?

What small daily actions will take you there?

Why it works: Your brain needs a strong emotional reason to chase a goal. Visualising it like a movie makes it real, vivid, and exciting. Something your mind wants to work towards!

The "20-Year-Old You vs. 80-Year-Old You" Duel - What advice would your older version of you give to your younger version?

Instructions:

Write two letters:

One from your 20-year-old self to your current self (if you're younger, think of your younger self's ambitions).

One from your 80-year-old self to your current self, giving wisdom from a life well-lived.

Compare the two letters. What did your 20-year-old self want that you might have forgotten? What regrets does your 80-year-old self warn you about?

Extract three key insights from these letters and turn them into tangible action points.

Why it works: It forces you to zoom out and see the bigger picture of your life. It helps you reconnect with your youthful ambitions while also keeping you accountable to your future self.

The "GPS System for Life" Exercise - if you don't set the destination, you'll end up wherever the road takes you!

Instructions:

Pick a BIG GOAL. Write it at the top of a page (Example: "Become financially free in 5 years").

Now, work backwards.

If you must reach this in 5 years, what must happen in 3 years?

What about 1 year from now?

What about 3 months from now?

And finally, what can you do this week to get started?

Write down the first small step and do it TODAY.

Why it works: Just like a GPS needs a final destination to chart a route, your mind needs a clear reverse-engineered plan to avoid getting lost.

The "One-Degree Shift" Challenge –Think of a plane flying from LA to New York, if it goes off course by just 1 degree, it will land in Washington D.C. instead of New York. Small changes create a massive impact over time!

Instructions:

Identify one habit that is slightly off course in your life. Example: "I waste 1 hour daily scrolling mindlessly on my phone."

"I hit the sleep button on my alarm every morning instead of waking up early."

Make a tiny shift instead of drastic changes.

Example: Instead of quitting social media completely, replace 10 minutes of scrolling with reading something useful.

Commit to 1-degree shifts every week for the next month. Track progress.

Why it works: Small, consistent improvements are more sustainable than extreme changes. A tiny change, maintained long enough, leads to massive results!

<u>The "Burn the Boats" Commitment Test -</u> When Alexander the Great landed on enemy shores, he burned his boats. His soldiers had no way back. They HAD to win. That's the power of full commitment!

Instructions:

Pick a serious goal that you've been half-hearted about. Example: "Starting my business."

"Getting fit and losing 10 kg."

Create a No-Excuse Commitment.

Announce it publicly (social media, friends, family).

Set a deadline.

Attach a consequence (Example: If I don't start my business by June, I'll donate ₹10,000 to a cause I dislike).

Why it works: When retreat is not an option, the only way is forward. This forces your brain to stay committed instead of quitting when things get hard.

<u>FINAL WORD:</u> Goals don't fail because they're impossible. They fail because they're vague, lack emotional connection, or don't have a real commitment mechanism

behind them. These exercises solve all that. Now, pick one, take action today, and let's get moving!

THE FINAL FRONTIER

UNLOCKING THE MIND

And here we are. After journeying through the intricate pathways of the mind, unravelling the mysteries of Beliefs, Emotions, Trauma, and Resilience, we arrive at a fundamental truth: Managing Expectations isn't about lowering them, but about approaching them with clarity and wisdom.

We've explored the brain, the silent architect of our perceptions, and the neurotransmitters that shape how we see and interpret the world. We've dissected belief systems, understanding how they take root and dictate what we consider possible. More importantly, we've learned how to challenge and reshape the beliefs that limit us.

We've walked through the powerful connection between emotions and expectations, discovering how emotional intelligence can help us respond rather than react. We've faced the weight of trauma, acknowledging its impact but also recognising the possibility of healing. Alongside, we've uncovered psychological complexes, those deeply ingrained patterns that subtly influence our self-worth and interactions, and found ways to free ourselves from their hold.

Through mindfulness, we've learned to embrace the present without being shackled by past disappointments or future anxieties. We've honed the art of communication, understanding that clarity and assertiveness can transform relationships and expectations alike. And above all, we've strengthened our resilience, realising that setbacks are not roadblocks but stepping stones to growth.

With real-world case studies, we've seen theory in action. With hands-on exercises, we've taken our learning from concept to practice. The question now is, what will you do with this knowledge? How will you reshape your expectations, recalibrate your mindset, and step into a world where you are in control of your own narrative?

This book was never meant to be just a collection of insights; it was meant to be a catalyst. A nudge. A challenge. And now, it totally depends on you what your next step will be.

Because life will continue to unfold in unpredictable ways. But now, you are equipped, not to control every outcome, but to navigate it all with newfound awareness, strength, and wisdom.

"उद्धरेदात्मनात्मानं नात्मानमवसादयेत्।आत्मैव ह्यात्मनो बन्धुरात्मैव रिपुरात्मनः॥*"Elevate yourself by your own mind; do not degrade yourself. For the mind is both a friend and an enemy to the self*

– Bhagavad Gita

Your Journey Continues: A Call to Growth

Personal growth isn't a destination; it's a continuous unfolding, an ever-expanding horizon. The work you've done while reading this book is just the beginning.

You've questioned old beliefs. You've examined the patterns that shaped you. You've confronted emotions, expectations, and the silent forces that influence your decisions. But now comes the real test - living it. Applying it. Making it second nature.

Will it be easy? Not always. Growth is messy. It's uncomfortable. It demands courage, the kind that nudges you to have difficult conversations, take risks, and embrace uncertainty. But here's the truth: everything you want, every transformation you seek, lies just beyond that discomfort.

So keep going. Keep questioning. Keep evolving. Consider resilience as though it is another muscle in your body, and overcome one challenge at a time. Practice mindfulness, not as an occasional exercise, but as a way of seeing, being, and responding. Speak your truth with clarity. Rewrite the expectations that no longer serve you. And above all, trust yourself.

Because you are more powerful than you think. Your mind, your emotions, your beliefs - they are not fixed. They are fluid, adaptable, and capable of extraordinary change. You are not bound by the past, nor by the stories you once told yourself.

So take this knowledge and run with it. Chase the version of yourself that is waiting beyond fear, beyond doubt. Keep growing, keep expanding, and keep embracing the life that is yours to shape. Because this is just the beginning…

EPILOGUE

WHERE WISDOM MEETS THE WORLD

The most dangerous moment is now - this quiet space between finishing the last page and deciding what happens next. Because real transformation doesn't live in concepts, but in the space where insight meets action.

You now hold something rare: the keys to your own freedom. Not theoretical freedom, but the kind that rewires how you experience Monday mornings, difficult conversations, and those 3 am, moments when old doubts come whispering. This is that crossroads where knowledge becomes power.

THE ALCHEMY OF ACTION

Great shifts happen in deceptively simple ways:

1. **The 24-Hour Crucible**: Identify one belief you're ready to release. Before tomorrow ends, take one concrete action that proves its opposite.

2. **Pattern Interrupts**: When you notice an old script running ("I can't...", "I'm not..."), pause. Ask: "What would my best self (wise and knowledgeable) do next?"
3. **Micro-Miracles**: Small, daily acts of courage compound faster than you imagine. That difficult email sent, that boundary held, that risk taken - these are the atoms of transformation.

YOUR LEGACY STARTS TODAY

History isn't made in grand declarations but in quiet moments of choosing differently. Every time you:

- Respond instead of react
- Question instead of assuming
- Create instead of criticising

You're not just changing a day - you're altering your trajectory.

THE INVITATION

This ending is your beginning. The world needs what you'll become when you stop holding back. Not a perfect version, but an authentic one. Not someone without fear, but someone who moves forward anyway.

Take a pen. Write these words on the first blank page you can find:

"Today I begin. Not when I'm ready. Not when it's easy. Now."

Then go make it true.

ABOUT THE AUTHOR

With over 30 years of experience in understanding, mentoring, and shaping people, Navneet Chandra is more than just a seasoned professional—he is a catalyst for transformation. Having navigated the complexities of human behavior across global landscapes—from the bustling corporate hubs of India to the dynamic business environments of the US and the Middle East—he brings a rich tapestry of insights into psychology, leadership, and organizational dynamics.

A certified Career Counsellor, Life Coach, Happiness Coach, proficient Psychometric analyst, a practitioner of REBT, CBT, Timeline Therapy, and NLP, Navneet has spent decades fine-tuning the art of expectation management, resilience, and emotional intelligence. Whether coaching top executives, mentoring young professionals, or delivering powerful training sessions, he has a unique ability to connect, influence, and inspire across all levels of an organization.

Having held senior management positions since 1998, Navneet thrives at the intersection of strategy and people, ensuring that raw potential is transformed into refined excellence. A firm believer in the power of mindful communication and self-awareness, he seamlessly blends real-world experience with psychological principles to help individuals and organizations achieve clarity, balance, and success.